NEW DIRECTIONS FOR EVALUATION
A Publication of the American Evaluation A

D0343378

Gary T. Henry, *Georgia State University*
EDITOR-IN-CHIEF

Jennifer C. Greene, *Cornell University*
EDITOR-IN-CHIEF

Using Performance Measurement to Improve Public and Nonprofit Programs

Kathryn E. Newcomer
The George Washington University

EDITOR

Number 75, Fall 1997

JOSSEY-BASS PUBLISHERS
San Francisco

USING PERFORMANCE MEASUREMENT TO IMPROVE PUBLIC AND
NONPROFIT PROGRAMS
Kathryn E. Newcomer (ed.)
New Directions for Evaluation, no. 75
Jennifer C. Greene, Gary T. Henry, Editors-in-Chief

Microfilm copies of issues and articles are available in 16mm and 35mm,
as well as microfiche in 105mm, through University Microfilms Inc., 300
North Zeeb Road, Ann Arbor, Michigan 48106-1346.

New Directions for Evaluation is indexed in Contents Pages in Education,
Higher Education Abstracts, and Sociological Abstracts.

ISSN 0164-7989   ISBN 0-7879-9846-X

NEW DIRECTIONS FOR EVALUATION is part of The Jossey-Bass Education
Series and is published quarterly by Jossey-Bass Inc., Publishers, 350
Sansome Street, San Francisco, California 94104-1342.

SUBSCRIPTIONS cost $63.00 for individuals and $105.00 for institutions,
agencies, and libraries. Prices subject to change.

EDITORIAL CORRESPONDENCE should be addressed to the Editors-in-Chief,
Jennifer C. Greene, Department of Policy Analysis and Management, MVR
Hall, Cornell University, Ithaca, NY 14853-4401, or Gary T. Henry,
School of Policy Studies, Georgia State University, P.O. Box 4039, Atlanta,
GA 30302-4039.

Jossey-Bass Web address: http://www.josseybass.com

EDITORIAL POLICY AND PROCEDURES

New Directions for Evaluation, a quarterly sourcebook, is an official publication of the American Evaluation Association. The journal publishes empirical, methodological, and theoretical works on all aspects of evaluation. A reflective approach to evaluation is an essential strand to be woven through every volume. The editors encourage volumes that have one of three foci: (1) craft volumes that present approaches, methods, or techniques that can be applied in evaluation practice, such as the use of templates, case studies, or survey research; (2) professional issue volumes that present issues of import for the field of evaluation, such as utilization of evaluation or locus of evaluation capacity; (3) societal issue volumes that draw out the implications of intellectual, social, or cultural developments for the field of evaluation, such as the women's movement, communitarianism, or multiculturalism. A wide range of substantive domains is appropriate for *New Directions for Evaluation;* however, the domains must be of interest to a large audience within the field of evaluation. We encourage a diversity of perspectives and experiences within each volume, as well as creative bridges between evaluation and other sectors of our collective lives.

The editors do not consider or publish unsolicited single manuscripts. Each issue of the journal is devoted to a single topic, with contributions solicited, organized, reviewed, and edited by a guest editor. Issues may take any of several forms, such as a series of related chapters, a debate, or a long article followed by brief critical commentaries. In all cases, the proposals must follow a specific format, which can be obtained from the editor-in-chief. These proposals are sent to members of the editorial board and to relevant substantive experts for peer review. The process may result in acceptance, a recommendation to revise and resubmit, or rejection. However, the editors are committed to working constructively with potential guest editors to help them develop acceptable proposals.

Jennifer C. Greene, Editor-in-Chief
Department of Policy Analysis and Management
MVR Hall
Cornell University
Ithaca, NY 14853-4401
e-mail: jcg8@cornell.edu

Gary T. Henry, Editor-in-Chief
School of Policy Studies
Georgia State University
P.O. Box 4039
Atlanta, GA 30302-4039
e-mail: gthenry@gsu.edu

CONTENTS

EDITOR'S NOTES

This volume critically reviews the current state of the art in the design and use of performance measurement in public and nonprofit programs. The context surrounding design and implementation of performance measurement systems is described, and best practices in performance measurement are discussed. Examples of the use of performance measurement in all levels of government and the nonprofit sector are provided. Guidance is also provided regarding use of performance measurement to improve applications of information technology and information systems.

Performance measurement is a very timely topic in the public and nonprofit sectors in the United States and in many countries around the world. Executive and legislative initiatives have required public managers to identify performance measures, set performance targets, and report on their progress. Funders have similarly asked nonprofits to show results for the support provided them. Program managers and budget officers have eagerly sought help in designing performance measurement strategies and systems. The Government Performance and Results Act of 1993, which calls for the use of performance measurement in virtually all federal agencies by the year 2000, has been deemed "the full employment act for program evaluators" due to the challenging measurement tasks presented. Program evaluators have much to offer current performance measurement efforts, especially in bringing stakeholders together to clarify program goals and determine how to best report results.

Although performance measurement is not new, the ubiquitous requirements for its use are. The specificity in identification of mission-based, outcome- or results-oriented measures has pushed program managers to think about program evaluation in a new light. Performance measurement is intended to be an institutionalized, routine process whereby the assessment of programmatic results can be undertaken in an ongoing fashion. Such institutionalization of evaluation processes has been promoted by program evaluation professionals, but the lack of resources and expertise has usually prohibited such ongoing monitoring.

Many conference papers on performance measurement have been presented at recent conferences of the American Evaluation Association, the American Society for Public Administration, and the International City Management Association, as well at as many national and regional training conferences. Much of the information published on performance measurement has been prescriptive, providing advice on how to approach the task, or anecdotal, recounting initial experiences with the process. Chapters in evaluation texts typically describe how performance measurement should be approached in a fairly theoretical fashion.

The authors of chapters in this volume include the most prominent experts on performance measurement in the federal government (Joseph S. Wholey) and local government (Harry P. Hatry), on the use of performance measures in the budgetary process (Philip G. Joyce), and on the use of performance measurement in information management (Sharon L. Caudle). Practitioners helping develop performance measurement systems (Michael Hendricks, Martha Taylor Greenway, Margaret C. Plantz, Cheryle A. Broom, and Marilyn Jackson) offer reality-based advice. With both practitioners and academics among the authors, the level of discussion about performance measurement is practical yet based on the theory underlying performance measurement.

This volume provides information on what actually works to ensure that performance measurement is useful for improving public programs. Lessons from case studies of the experience of pilot programs undertaken in response to the Government Performance and Results Act of 1993 are offered here. Field experience with performance measurement at all levels of government and in the nonprofit sector is used to offer advice on what works and what does not. Chapter Five, on measuring the performance of information technology and information systems, draws on the author's experience with public agencies across the country to provide concrete recommendations. Also, lessons about what useful training involves are drawn from performance measurement training. The coverage of issues regarding the design and use of performance measurement systems is aimed at program managers in all areas of governmental and nonprofit service delivery—from health to education to national defense.

Chapter One sets the stage for the volume by describing what performance measurement involves and identifying the key challenges managers face in designing and using performance measurement systems. Guidance on how the evaluation profession might contribute to performance measurement efforts is offered.

In Chapter Two, Margaret C. Plantz, Martha Taylor Greenway, and Michael Hendricks outline the scope of performance measurement in the nonprofit health and human services sector. The ways performance measures are used by national oversight organizations, managed-care companies, and accrediting bodies are described. The authors draw on their field experience with outcome measurement for nonprofits to offer thirty useful lessons on developing and using outcome findings.

Harry P. Hatry provides an overview of current developments affecting the use of performance measurement at the local level of government, in Chapter Three. He identifies specific arrangements, such as performance-based partnerships, that constitute relatively new arenas for performance measurement, and he discusses how measurement should relate to program evaluation.

Philip G. Joyce addresses the role that performance measures can and do play in budgeting, in Chapter Four. He places performance-based budgeting into historical context and describes factors currently constraining use of performance measures for resource allocation purposes.

In Chapter Five, Sharon L. Caudle describes how performance of information technology (IT) can be measured and analyzed most effectively. She outlines five best practices in IT performance management and offers detailed suggestions on how to implement useful performance measurement systems.

Cheryle A. Broom and Marilyn Jackson draw from their own extensive experience as trainers, in Chapter Six. They offer advice on how to design and implement effective training to the many different sorts of stakeholders interested in using performance measurement to improve government programs.

Joseph S. Wholey and I conclude the volume, in Chapter Seven, by drawing from experience with performance measurement in the U.S. federal government to make recommendations as to how evaluators can apply their skills to help define, measure, and improve government performance.

This volume would never have materialized had it not been for Joe Wholey. Joe Wholey has been a key architect of both the theory and practice of performance measurement, and he has had a tremendous impact on all of us interested in the topic. Thank you, Joe, for all the intellectual inspiration and moral support you have given me for over a decade.

My thanks go to all of the authors who contributed to this volume, especially to Sharon Caudle, who also served as a reviewer of much of the volume. We all thank our reviewers—Sharon Caudle, Ron Carlee, Ron Sanders, Bernard Pitsvada, Jill Moses, and, most of all, Lois-ellin Datta. One could not find a more supportive series editor than Lois. And, finally, thanks to Roy Wright for helping me put this all together.

Kathryn E. Newcomer
Editor

KATHRYN E. NEWCOMER is professor and chair in the Department of Public Administration at The George Washington University, Washington, D.C.

*An unprecedented challenge to the evaluation profession has arisen
from the increasing demand for documentation of results of public and
nonprofit programs. The current status of performance measurement
efforts is described in this chapter, and many challenges facing
program managers and other users of performance data are identified.*

Using Performance Measurement to Improve Programs

Kathryn E. Newcomer

A variety of initiatives undertaken by federal, state, and local elected officials during the last two decades have required that public managers provide evidence that their programs work. Program managers around the world, from Sydney, Australia to Sunnyvale, California, have been asked to document the results of their work. Although program effectiveness has been questioned before, current demands have been more focused, requesting both specific performance measures and targets. Funders in the nonprofit world have similarly become more insistent and focused in their requests for documentation of results. An unprecedented challenge to the evaluation profession has arisen out of this severe imbalance between demand for and supply of performance data.

Performance measurement is the label typically given the many efforts undertaken within governments and in the nonprofit sector to meet the new demand for documentation of results (Wholey and Hatry, 1992). Different stakeholders involved with programs funded by public and nonprofit sources hold different ideas about what constitutes satisfactory performance, but much of the guidance provided to program managers indicates that the intended outcomes of the programs are what should be monitored (Government Performance and Results Act of 1993; U.S. Office of Management and Budget, 1996; and Hatry, H., van Houten, T., Plantz, M. C., and Greenway, M. T., 1996.)

Assessment of service delivery at the local level of government is not new, but linking the measures, or indicators, to program mission; setting performance targets; and regularly reporting on the achievement of target levels of performance are new features in the performance measurement movement sweeping across the public and nonprofit sectors in the United States. With program managers rushing to meet deadlines regarding development of performance measures and collection systems, questions about the effectiveness of these efforts are appropriate. What is needed to design and support an effective performance measurement system? What does effective performance measurement entail? Why is demand so far outrunning supply in this blossoming field of program evaluation?

This chapter reviews the state of the art in performance measurement. The relationship between performance measurement and program evaluation is discussed. Some of the most pressing issues and challenges facing program managers and all users of performance data are identified.

Measuring the Performance of Public and Nonprofit Programs

Programmatic performance is not an objective reality to be measured and evaluated. Performance is a socially constructed reality (Berger and Luckmann, 1967). Criteria for defining and rating a program's performance must be assembled and agreed upon by a group of officials with both the authority and responsibility for the task. With public and nonprofit programs there are many stakeholders with interests in the performance of the program, from those receiving benefits to those allocating funding, and they may value potential criteria differently.

Traditionally, *inputs,* or the resources allocated to the delivery of programs, have been measured to track programs. Traditional process-oriented management techniques in both the public and nonprofit sectors have traced budgetary and staffing figures to assess how programs are faring. Evaluation activities during the last twenty years have gone beyond basic budgetary monitoring to count program *outputs,* such as products and services delivered to clients or activities funded. Implementation evaluation has focused attention, for example, on counting outputs and assessing whether or not the outputs have been delivered as intended in legislative and regulatory guidance.

Measurement of some outputs, such as counting the number of children immunized, captures the intended result of the program. More typically, counting outputs does not convey whether or not persons, households, schools, or other institutions have been affected in the manner intended in the program's mission. *Outcome* is the term reserved for the result desired by the program's designers.

Program outcomes are the intended results of programs that many of those currently demanding evidence of the value added by programs want to see. *Outcome monitoring,* or the routine measurement and reporting of indicators of outcome-oriented results of programs, is another term that has been used to express the measurement of the outcome facet of program performance (Affholter, 1994). Outcomes may be usefully differentiated by whether or not they are *intermediate* or *end outcomes.* Intermediate outcomes include immediate reactions of clients, for example, satisfaction with training or with medical care, and actions taken by other levels of government or by those in the non-profit or private sector. For example, firms implementing pollution control procedures upon intervention by the federal or state environmental protection agency may constitute an intermediate outcome of that agency.

End outcomes, or impacts, are the intended results of the program upon persons or society. For example, a person's or group's health and the air and water quality affected by regulated firms are end outcomes of the health and environmental protection programs. However, such things as health and air and water quality are affected by many things out of the control of the government, so it is the net impact of the program upon such phenomena, when other influences are discounted, that constitutes the intended program outcome.

It should be noted that community-level or social indicators such as teenage pregnancy rates and crime rates sometimes serve as performance measures for state and local governments. For example, Oregon's milestones and benchmarking effort has used social indicators to set state performance targets (U.S. General Accounting Office, 1994). However, the vast majority of performance measurement efforts focus at the level of an organization or program in identifying indicators of performance.

Selecting What to Measure

Performance measurement is a fairly inclusive term that may refer to the routine measurement of program inputs, outputs, intermediate outcomes, or end outcomes. Decisions about what to measure reflect two key factors: the *intended use* of the performance data and the *value priorities* of those stakeholders who choose what to measure. Performance data can be used to support a variety of decisions, and perceptions about which decisions will be affected are critical to those charged with selecting performance measures. The relative priority given to values such as efficiency, equity, and service quality, among others, also affects the selection of indicators.

Reflecting the signals emanating from citizen revolts and legislative and executive demands for evidence that programs work, most governmental calls for performance measures suggest that the measures will inform resource allocation decisions. At the federal level of government, for example, the Office of Management and Budget (OMB) has requested that agencies provide performance measures with their budgetary submissions for the past five years. OMB has sent messages through many of their initiatives that performance measures must support budgetary requests and that they can be used defensively in budget-cutting exercises. The Government Performance and Results Act of 1993 (the Results Act) has also sent the message that through planning and performance measurement government managers can "improve the confidence of the American people in the capability of the federal government by systematically holding federal agencies accountable for achieving program results, and . . . improve federal program effectiveness and public accountability by promoting a new focus on results, service quality and customer satisfaction." The Results Act also adds that internal management should be improved through performance measurement, but the focus on accountability, accompanied by signals from OMB, indicates that resource allocation is the primary, if not driving, use for the performance data.

Pushing performance measurement as a tool to assess managerial accountability actually implies both that managers should use the performance data to demonstrate that the money allocated to their programs has been well spent, and to improve the operations of the programs they manage. But can the same performance data be used for both purposes?

There is a significant dilemma posed by attempting to identify and collect performance data for two vastly different uses. In the evaluation profession the distinction between formative, or process, evaluation and summative evaluation is pertinent. Formative evaluations collect data about the extent or nature of program implementation. Summative evaluations collect data to assess whether or not the program has the intended impact (Scriven, 1967; Scheirer, 1994). When questions are directed toward improving program administration, certain data will be relevant. However, very different data will be relevant for decisions regarding whether or not a program should continue to receive funding at a steady level—or at all. Evaluators interested in maximizing the use of evaluation data long have stressed the importance of matching the data collected to the intended use (Patton, 1986).

Managers pressed to choose performance measures during lean budgetary times, when they typically have very limited resources for performance measurement, face a tough choice. Strategically selecting measures that will make a program look effective to funders is a likely outcome. In many cases the sorts of measures that might effectively inform program improvement decisions may provide data that managers would not find helpful for resource allocation purposes. Given a choice about the use of limited resources to develop performance measurement systems, collecting data that will support budgetary requests will probably win out over collecting internally useful, but less resource supportive, data.

Another interesting dilemma currently facing public and nonprofit managers is that the intended use for the performance data is not clear. Given the mixed messages typical of political pronouncements that performance measurement should be used to improve both the programs and the budgetary process, there may be a lack of clarity about potential use, with resulting anxiety among program managers about what to measure. Political requestors, such as mayors and city councils, may press for data that will show the public what they are getting, whereas city managers and other career managers call for internally useful data. Two or more clear signals can become confusing when line managers are trying to adhere to conflicting guidance.

Many stakeholders are involved in selecting performance measures, and they bring different values to the table. Programs delivered in both the public and nonprofit sectors have multiple constituencies and, typically, multiple objectives. Programs are designed to achieve specific goals, such as improving the health or employability of beneficiaries, but they are also intended to be delivered in an efficient, equitable, customer-friendly, environmentally sound, and fair manner. In other words, there are many values attached to service delivery in the public and nonprofit sectors, and different stakeholders will prioritize these values differently as they choose what to measure.

Simply forging a consensus among diverse stakeholders with the authority to choose what to measure is no small feat. For example, within public agencies and nongovernmental organizations and foundations, staff in budget, financial management, and development offices view the world differently than line managers, yet they may share responsibility for envisioning performance, and appropriate measures of it, with the managers.

Donald Kettl (1996) has aptly noted that one key benefit to be derived from implementing performance measurement in the federal government is improved communication. Envisioning program missions, strategic objectives, and performance measures that will measure the extent to which objectives are met requires that many stakeholders within agencies and across governmental organizations, such as OMB, congressional committees, and the agencies, come to agreement on appropriate measurement strategies. Such horizontal and vertical communication is not easy to facilitate but is rewarding for programs bolstered by stakeholder agreement.

Performance Measurement as Program Evaluation

Program evaluation professionals might well be thrilled at the widespread calls for measurement of programmatic results to inform decision making. In fact, when initially passed, the federal Government Performance and Results Act was dubbed the "full employment act for program evaluators." If government agencies had reinvigorated evaluation offices and used program evaluators to help design their performance measurement systems, all parties would have benefited. This typically has not been the case.

How does performance measurement relate to program evaluation? Program evaluation is clearly the more inclusive of the two approaches to reviewing programs in the public and nonprofit sectors. Program evaluation consists of the systematic description and judgment of programs and, to the extent feasible, systematic assessment of the extent to which they have the intended results (Wholey, Hatry, and Newcomer, 1994). Evaluation efforts may focus on program inputs, operations, or results.

Program evaluation is retrospective, collecting and analyzing information on existing programs. The specific evaluation strategy employed reflects who wants to know what about a program as well as who collects the information. There is great variety in the types of evaluation questions raised by program management and oversight bodies, ranging from problem-based investigations to performance assessments to evaluations of the net impact of programs (Newcomer, 1996). Evaluation efforts are currently undertaken in many inspector general offices at the federal level, as well as by legislative audit offices and comptroller offices at state and local levels of government in the United States, and by evaluation consultants within and outside of government.

Evaluators can and often do address challenging "why" and "how" questions with program evaluation methods. Why are programs not delivering the expected results? Why does implementation of the same program vary across sites? How do specific program components contribute to outcomes achieved? Why are unintended negative and positive results occurring? Performance measurement typically captures quantitative indicators that tell what is occurring with regard to program outputs and perhaps outcomes but, in itself, will not address the how and why questions. Certainly, in some circumstances budgetary oversight bodies may not be interested in the how and why questions; they just want to know how many or how much has been delivered. But if internal management wants to know how to improve program operations, they must venture beyond the performance data.

Useful comparisons of disaggregated performance data can instruct management on program operations. Comparative analyses of client data, as well as case studies of delivery sites, are also important services program evaluators can provide. Addressing questions about quality assurance for services contracted out can and should be undertaken by program evaluators; current trends toward more privatization of governmental services make oversight of such services even more important.

Can program evaluation professionals support performance measurement efforts? Absolutely! Will these complementary efforts evolve naturally? Probably not. Only if those charged with using performance measurement systems recognize what they can learn and what they cannot learn from the performance data themselves will program evaluation be drawn on to support and strengthen performance measurement systems.

Challenges to Effective Use of Performance Measurement

The demand for performance data to demonstrate program results in agencies and nonprofits offering all sorts of services is high. What impediments currently appear to constrain the supply of useful performance data? Some of the political and communications challenges in choosing what to measure have been discussed here. More issues are raised in the chapters to follow. Exhibit 1.1 summarizes the major challenges that currently constrain the effectiveness of performance measurement in improving programs.

Abundant political support and resources are essential to ensure that performance measurement systems are designed with adequate input from key stakeholders and with technical expertise to ensure useful systems. Consultation with stakeholders in oversight bodies, service beneficiaries, and internal staff takes time and resource support. Adequate technical assistance to support

Exhibit 1.1. Challenges to Using Performance Measurements to Improve Programs in the Public and Nonprofit Sectors

1. What should be measured?
    What decisions will the measures inform?
    Whose decisions will the measures inform?
    Who will select the measures?
    What values will be served by the measures?
2. Where are the resources to support measurement systems?
    Where will the performance measurement system be maintained?
    Where are the resources for system design and maintenance?
    Will top-level management ensure continued resource support?
    Where are the individual and program-level incentives to support and use performance measurement systems?
3. How will program evaluation be used to support performance measurement?
    Is there political will to support efforts to learn why program results were or were not achieved?
    Is there political will to support efforts to learn how to improve programs?
    Where are the resources to support program evaluation efforts?
4. Why are discrepancies between expectations and outcomes of performance measurement likely?
    What sorts of technical assistance to facilitate design of performance measurement systems are needed and available?
    Where is there potential for mixed signals about the use of performance measurement in decision making?
    What are likely consequences of mixed signals about the use of performance measurement in decision making?
    Why might performance measures inadequately capture program results?

both design and implementation is essential. The availability of both political and technical support should not always be assumed.

Expectations that performance measurement is attainable and will be useful are fairly high. It is certainly feasible that reasonable indicators of program outputs, and perhaps intermediate outcomes, can be routinely collected. Success stories about the use of performance measurement to support resource requests and to convince the public of the value of local government services in the United States abound (Epstein and Olsen, 1996; also see Chapter Three of this volume). Why might outcomes of measurement efforts fail to meet these raised expectations?

Factors that may hinder effective utilization of performance measurement to support decision making are political and communication challenges with which program evaluators are quite familiar. So, what advice might the evaluation profession offer to managers charged with devising useful performance measurement systems?

First, designing a performance measurement system is an extremely time- and resource-consuming process that should be undertaken with clear expectations among relevant parties about what is needed. Political will from the top of the pertinent organizations, whether that be a city or county council or a department secretary, must be in place to secure the necessary resources and political commitment from stakeholders. In the development process, multiple stakeholders involved with programs must work together to come to agreement on programmatic mission and objectives, on the potential use of performance measures, and on the set of performance indicators that will be most useful to them.

Second, defining performance is an inherently political process. It is also an inherently governmental process. Elected representatives and their agents create and authorize programs. Knowledge of legislative history and program intent is essential to ensure that program objectives and performance measures accurately reflect the intent of the program creators. There are no correct answers when it comes to selecting performance measures. The "right" measures are so defined by those stakeholders who hold the most influence over the process. Smart consultants can help facilitate useful development processes, but they will not be able to identify performance measures. Sharp trainers cannot guarantee that their trainees will be better able to select the correct measures, either. Knowledge of the political context is more valuable than methodological expertise in this endeavor, though both are necessary skills. Concepts of performance and the most useful measures of it will evolve. Flexibility to change how performance is measured must be assured, so that systems can be upgraded and improved over time.

Third, location of a performance measurement system matters. Financial management, policy, and planning and budget offices all have stakes in the development of performance measures, but they should probably not manage the system. Line managers should be empowered to develop and use the systems. They need to take ownership over the systems so that they will be willing and able to use them. There must be adequate financial support so that performance measurement does not get relegated to line managers without resources. As additional yet uncompensated work, data collection to support performance measurement will simply not get done. Authority and resources must accompany responsibility for performance measurement.

Fourth, there must be clear communication about the use of performance measures within the relevant political organizations. Key political stakeholders, such as city councils and city manager offices, departmental budget offices, and congressional committees, must be brought together to discuss use before commitments to specific measures are made. Mixed signals or fear of punitive use can undercut line management commitment to performance measurement quickly. Even rumors of punitive use of performance measures can wreak quick damage.

Fifth, program evaluators with substantive expertise in service areas can add value to both design and use of performance measurement. Evaluators can educate potential users on pertinent distinctions. They can offer program logic modeling to help distinguish outputs from intermediate outcomes and from end outcomes. They can demonstrate the problems in drawing causal linkages between programs and end outcomes affected by many factors out of the control of the programs. They can identify the costs and benefits of different data collection approaches for capturing programmatic outputs and outcomes. They can point to likely implementation traps, such as not providing adequate political leadership and technical support for system maintenance. And they can help moderate expectations to help reduce disappointment when measurement supporters find that performance data are not used directly in decision making. Twenty years of discussion about how to enhance utilization of evaluation has taught evaluators many valuable lessons quite pertinent to current developments in performance measurement. Our knowledge about such things as the criticality of adequate consultation with users and the involvement of stakeholders in every phase of evaluation efforts—from design to use—and the importance of audience-oriented presentation can certainly inform current performance measurement efforts. Performance measurement is but one facet of program evaluation, and it can be well served by the evaluation profession's institutional memory about enhancing utilization of strong performance data.

References

Affholter, D. P. "Outcome Monitoring." In J. Wholey, H. P. Hatry, and K. E. Newcomer (eds.), *Handbook of Practical Program Evaluation*. San Francisco: Jossey-Bass, 1994.

Berger, P. L., and Luckmann, T. *The Social Construction of Reality*. Garden City, N.Y.: Anchor Books, 1967.

Epstein, J., and Olsen, R. T. "Lessons Learned by State and Local Governments." *The Public Manager*, 1996, 25 (3), 41–44.

Hatry, H. P., Sullivan, J. M., Fountain, J. R., Jr., and Kremer, L. (eds.). *Service Efforts and Accomplishment Reporting: Its Time Has Come—An Overview*. Norwalk, Conn.: Government Accounting Standards Board, 1990.

Hatry, H., van Houten, T., Plantz, M. C., and Greenway, M. T. *Measuring Program Outcomes: A Practical Approach*. Alexandria, Va.: United Way of America, 1996.

Kettl, D. F. "Implementation of the Government Performance and Results Act of 1993." Testimony before a joint hearing of the House Committee on Government Reform and Oversight and the Senate Committee on Governmental Affairs, Mar. 6, 1996, 104th Congress.

Newcomer, K. E. "Evaluating Public Programs." In J. L. Perry (ed.), *Handbook of Public Administration*. (2nd ed.) San Francisco: Jossey-Bass, 1996.

Patton, M. Q. *Utilization of Focused Evaluation*. Newbury Park, Calif.: Sage, 1986.

Scheirer, M. A. "Designing and Using Process Evaluation. In J. Wholey, H. P. Hatry, and K. E. Newcomer (eds.), *Handbook of Practical Program Evaluation*. San Francisco: Jossey-Bass, 1994.

Scriven, M. "The Methodology of Evaluation." In R. W. Tyler, R. M. Gagne, and M. Scriven (eds.), *Perspectives on Curriculum Evaluation*. American Educational Research Association Monograph Series on Curriculum Evaluation, no. 1. Chicago: Rand McNally, 1967.

Shadis, W. R., Cook, T. D., and Leviton, L. C. *Foundations of Program Evaluation*. Newbury Park, Calif.: Sage, 1991.

U.S. General Accounting Office. *Managing for Results: State Experiences Provide Insights for Federal Management Reform*. GAO/GGD-95-22. Washington, D.C.: General Accounting Office, 1994.

U.S. Office of Management and Budget. *Preparation and Submission of Budget Estimates*. Circular A-11. Washington, D.C.: Office of Management and Budget, 1996.

Wholey, J. S., and Hatry, H. P. "The Case for Performance Monitoring." *Public Administration Review*, 1992, 5 (6), 604–610.

Wholey, J. S., Hatry, H. P., and Newcomer, K. E. (eds.). *Handbook of Practical Program Evaluation*. San Francisco: Jossey-Bass, 1994.

KATHRYN E. NEWCOMER is professor and chair in the Department of Public Administration, The George Washington University, Washington, D.C.

Like their counterparts in the public sector, managers of nonprofit agencies are aggressively measuring the outcomes of their efforts. This chapter describes current activities in five important areas, offers thirty useful lessons, and discusses seven key challenges still to be overcome. These insights from the nonprofit sector are equally useful to persons working in other settings.

Outcome Measurement: Showing Results in the Nonprofit Sector

Margaret C. Plantz, Martha Taylor Greenway, Michael Hendricks

Other chapters in this volume discuss approaches to performance measurement in government settings. The nonprofit sector is also active in this area and is currently focusing its attention on a relatively new aspect of performance monitoring: outcome measurement.

This chapter summarizes the history of performance measurement in the nonprofit health and human services sector and defines key concepts in outcome measurement. It reports on activities in five key areas and describes thirty lessons the field has learned from those who have led the way. Finally it identifies seven pressing challenges that lie ahead.

Background: Performance Measurement in the Nonprofit Sector

There are approximately 495,000 tax-exempt organizations in the United States (excluding churches) that may receive tax-deductible contributions. Of those with incomes above $25,000, roughly 55,000 are classified as human service organizations, and another 28,000 are health related (Hodgkinson and Weitzman, 1996). In this chapter, the term *nonprofits* refers to these health and human service organizations. The types of health and human services that nonprofit organizations provide include housing and residential care, youth development, recreation, services to children and families, employment assistance, crime and delinquency prevention, food and nutrition, and substance abuse and addiction treatment (Hodgkinson and Weitzman, 1996).

Nonprofits may receive tax-deductible contributions from individuals, companies, and foundations. In addition, they often receive fees for services and government funds. The latter generally are a mix of federal and state dollars that flow from a federally legislated program. In 1992, for example, government grants accounted for 24 percent of revenues to human service organizations (Hodgkinson and Weitzman, 1996).

The nonprofit sector has been measuring certain aspects of performance for twenty-five years or more. During that period, the scope of performance measurement has expanded to address such issues as

Financial accountability. The first focus of nonprofit performance measurement was documenting how funds are spent. Early guidelines included *Standards of Accounting and Financial Reporting for Voluntary Health and Welfare Organizations* (National Health Council and National Assembly for Social Policy and Development, 1964) and *Accounting and Financial Reporting* (United Way of America, 1974).

Program products, or *outputs.* Shortly after starting to measure how funds were spent, agencies began to measure what the funds generated. Generally, output measures are measures of volume in two categories: products delivered (such as numbers of counseling sessions held, brochures distributed, days of care provided) and people served. Twenty years ago, for example, United Way of America's program classification system defined 587 human service categories and suggested product measures for each (United Way of America, 1976).

Adherence to standards of quality in service delivery. Concerns with service delivery issues such as staff qualifications, staff-to-client ratios, specific service delivery practices, record keeping, confidentiality protections, and condition of facilities led to the formation of accreditation and certification groups. The Council on Accreditation of Services for Families and Children, formed in 1977, was one of the first independent accrediting bodies.

Participant-related measures. In the 1980s, funders began seeking assurance that agencies provided services to those most in need. This prompted collection and reporting of client data, including demographic characteristics (such as age, income, race or ethnicity, gender, marital status, and area of residence) and information about the client's problem or status prior to service.

Key performance indicators. Several public accounting firms created performance measures for nonprofits. These indicators were largely ratios among various categories of inputs, services, outputs, and total costs. Peat Marwick produced a seminal resource in this area (Elkin and Molitor, 1984).

Client satisfaction. Later in the 1980s, accrediting bodies began requiring services to measure participant satisfaction as an additional element of quality assurance. Elements of satisfaction included physical and cultural accessibility, timeliness, courteousness, physical condition of facilities, and overall satisfaction.

By 1990, the nonprofit sector was commonly measuring all of these aspects of performance except client satisfaction (Taylor and Sumariwalla,

1993) and these measures yielded critical information about the services non-profits were providing. Increasingly, however, there has been recognition that, although such measures show how much effort has been generated for how many individuals, they reveal nothing about whether this effort has made any difference—whether anyone is better off as a result of the service. Outcome measurement responds to this gap.

The measurement of a program's outcomes—the benefits or results it has for its customers, clients, or participants—can and will have a tremendous impact on nonprofit health and human service organizations. Outcome measurement shifts the focus from activities to results, from how a program operates to the good it accomplishes. Information on the extent to which program participants are having the intended outcomes is powerful and useful feedback. Managers of nonprofit organizations that already have implemented outcome measurement report that

- A clear definition of the program's intended outcomes, in itself, provides focus for the program's work.
- Understanding their current level of outcome achievement provides a barometer to assess progress and direct future activities.
- Outcome measurement provides invaluable information to improve programs and see if the improvements make the intended difference.
- Outcome information is a powerful motivator of staff, who now can observe the progress they are making with participants in a consistent, tangible manner.
- It becomes a powerful recruitment tool for volunteers who have many other choices for how they spend their time.
- It helps position the agency in the community as a successful organization, which in turn leads to increased promotion and financial support (Hatry, van Houten, Plantz, and Greenway, 1996).

Introducing Outcome Measurement

The United Way of America manual, *Measuring Program Outcomes: A Practical Approach* (Hatry, van Houten, Plantz, and Greenway, 1996), defines program outcomes as "benefits or changes for participants during or after their involvement with a program" (p. 2). Merely attending the program does not represent an outcome. An outcome is something that the program participant is, has, or does in response to the service provided. An outcome is distinct from program output, which is the number of units of service delivered or the number of people served. In other words, outputs are about the *program,* whereas outcomes are about the *participants.*

Outcomes are usually benefits or changes in participants' knowledge, attitudes, values, skills, behavior, condition, or status. Most often, an outcome represents a change for the better, although the outcome for some programs is that participants get worse more slowly than they would have otherwise. Examples of outcomes are that participants

- Know the daily nutritional requirements for a pregnant woman (knowledge)
- Recognize that school achievement is necessary to future success (attitude)
- Believe that cheating on a test is wrong (value)
- Are able to read at the sixth-grade level (skill)
- Use verbal rather than physical means to resolve conflict (behavior)
- Have improved health (condition)
- Reside in a permanent, independent setting (status)

In many cases there is not just one desired outcome for participants, but a series of outcomes, with one outcome contributing to another. This hierarchy of logically related changes or benefits comprises a series of *if-then* relationships. For example, *if* a program provides prenatal counseling to pregnant teens, *then* the teens have increased knowledge of good prenatal care. *If* the teens have increased knowledge of good prenatal care, *then* this leads to changed behavior: The teens eat the proper foods; take a prenatal vitamin each day; and avoid cigarettes, alcohol, and other drugs. *If* the teens follow these practices, *then* the result is that the teens deliver healthy newborns.

This hierarchy of program outcomes describes the logic or theory of how the program brings about benefits for participants. Figure 2.1 depicts the conceptual chain of influences, with program inputs (resources) leading to activities, which lead to outputs, which lead to a series of outcomes. The figure shows three levels of outcomes—initial, intermediate, and longer-term—although the number and terminology are not as important as the concept of a logically linked series of changes.

The farther one goes on this if-then chain beyond a program's outputs, the less influence the program has on the achievement of the outcome and the more likely it is that other forces will intervene. In the previous example, the program can directly influence the initial outcome of the pregnant teens' knowledge of good prenatal practices. In contrast, the teens' general health when they became pregnant and their involvement with drugs before coming to the program—neither of which the program can control—may have as much influence as the program on the longer-term outcome of delivering healthy infants.

A recurring, and vexing, issue in outcome measurement is deciding how far out the outcome chain a program should go in selecting its longest-term outcome. This decision requires a balance between two needs:

The longest-term outcome must be far enough out on the if-then chain to capture meaningful change for participants and reflect the full extent of the program's benefit for them. For the program just mentioned, participants knowing what constitutes good prenatal care is an important link in the if-then chain, but it is not meaningful as an end in itself and is not all the program aspires to achieve for participants. The program needs to go beyond that initial outcome in measuring its benefits.

On the other hand, the longest-term outcome should not be so far out on the if-then chain that the program's influence is washed out by other factors. It must be rea-

Figure 2.1. Inputs Through Outcomes: The Conceptual Chain

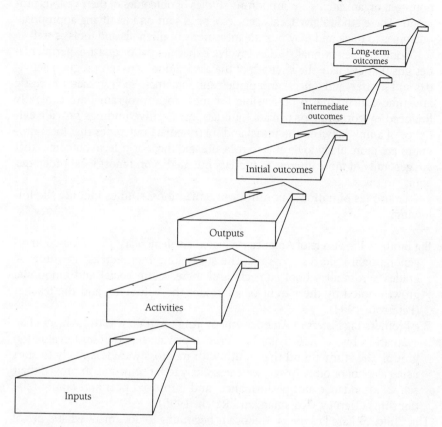

sonable to believe that the program can influence the longest-term outcome in a nontrivial way, even though it cannot control it. In the program described earlier, contact with the teenage mothers ends when their infants are born. Extending the program logic chain from the outcome of healthy births to an even longer-term outcome of "the children are developmentally on target at age two" is not sound in view of all the other factors that will influence mothers and babies in the intervening two years.

Recent Developments in the Nonprofit Sector

The past few years have seen an explosion of outcome measurement activity in the nonprofit sector. Several national organizations have set out to both measure program outcomes and provide resources to help local affiliate agencies measure their own outcomes. The rise of the managed-care industry and the expansion of accreditation and certification criteria to include outcome measurement are lending urgency to some of these efforts. The following examples illustrate five prominent areas of activity.

National organizations are conducting research on outcomes. Several national nonprofit organizations are supporting studies of outcomes of their various programs. These studies give local agencies a head start on identifying appropriate outcomes to track and may provide measurement methods and tools as well.

Some of the national studies involve experimental or quasi-experimental designs that evaluate the strength of the association between program activities and shorter- and longer-term participant outcomes. Such studies, too costly and time-consuming to be feasible for most local programs, are generally financed by corporate or private foundations. Positive findings provide evidence of a link between the initial and intermediate outcomes that local programs are more likely to be able to measure and the longer-term outcomes that are generally of more interest to funders but are beyond most local programs' ability to track.

Examples of national nonprofit organizations' studies include the following:

Big Brothers Big Sisters of America evaluated an elementary school-based intergenerational linkages program. The study found an increase in students' grades across all school subjects and increases in social and emotional growth noted by the parent or guardian, the volunteer, and the teacher (Peterson, 1994).

Big Brothers Big Sisters of America's mentoring program was the subject of an evaluation by Public/Private Ventures, a private research and evaluation group. The study found that youth with mentors were less likely to start using alcohol or other drugs, were less likely to hit someone, improved their school attendance and performance, and improved peer and family relationships (Tierney, Grossman, and Resch, 1995).

The Child Welfare League of America is beginning to document what types of settings and services are related to what outcomes for what kinds of children and youth. The study will track both shorter-term outcomes—such as placements into less-intensive settings, family reunification, educational achievement, and behavioral problems—and longer-term outcomes—such as employment, contacts with juvenile and criminal justice systems, and use of alcohol and other drugs (Child Welfare League of America, 1995).

Girl Scouts of the U.S.A. commissioned Louis Harris and Associates to study outcomes of Girl Scouting. Girl Scouts had better grades than a comparison group; were more actively involved in extracurricular activities; and were less likely to say they would cheat on a test, engage in sexual activity, and drink alcohol (Brown and Conn, 1990).

Girls Incorporated examined the effects of four age-targeted adolescent pregnancy prevention programs. The study found that the programs reduced the onset of intercourse, increased use of contraception for girls who were sexually active, and decreased pregnancy (Nicholson, Postrada, and Weiss, 1991).

Girls Incorporated also evaluated its substance abuse prevention program. Results showed that program participants were more likely to leave situations where peers were using harmful substances and had less favorable attitudes toward drinking alcohol. The program reduced incidence of drinking among participants and delayed the onset of drinking among participants who had not previously drunk alcohol (Jacobs, Nicholson, Plotch, and Weiss, 1993).

National organizations are developing resources for local agencies. A number of national organizations are developing outcome measurement tools to help local program managers monitor the extent to which program participants achieve the changes the programs intend. In the ideal case, the outcomes, indicators, measurement approaches, and other materials derive from experimental research linking an intervention to specific outcomes. In all cases, however, nationally developed resources save local programs a significant amount of time and effort and often bring to bear a level of expertise most local programs cannot access independently. Recently published resources include the following:

Boy Scouts of America has produced *Scouting's Positive Impact on the Community* (1996). Developed in response to local United Way organizations' increasing requests for funded agencies to document program outcomes, the publication gives guidance on presenting the Scouting program within an outcome measurement framework.

Girls Incorporated has published *Assess for Success* (Frederick and Nicholson, 1991). The manual provides an overview of outcome measurement concepts, as well as instructions and data collection instruments for observing girls' behavior and surveying girls and parents about girls' outcomes. The instruments are program-specific and age-targeted.

Goodwill Industries International's report, *Program Evaluation: Guidelines for Development and Implementation* (1994), describes a program evaluation system that incorporates outcome measurement. It includes guidelines for developing outcomes and includes examples of specific outcome indicators.

United Way of America has published *Measuring Program Outcomes: A Practical Approach* (Hatry, van Houten, Plantz, and Greenway, 1996), a manual for any nonprofit human service agency seeking to develop an outcome measurement system. It offers a step-by-step process for identifying outcomes, indicators, and data collection methods and for reporting and using data. Quotes and vignettes from more than thirty agencies that have implemented outcome measurement offer insights from the field. The manual does not give program-specific outcome indicators or data collection methods.

Additional resources are in development. For example:

The American Red Cross is convening representatives of local affiliates to develop program logic models with suggested outcomes and indicators for core national programs such as disaster relief.

Big Brothers Big Sisters of America is developing outcome measurement methods and tools for their affiliates based on the study by Public/Private Ventures described earlier.

Girl Scouts of the U.S.A. has engaged a national evaluator who, through focus groups with participants and an extensive literature review, has identified measurable outcomes for Girl Scouting programs and has developed survey instruments and data analysis software for local councils across the country to use.

The YMCA of the USA is taking a similar approach, working with the Search Institute to develop ten survey modules of aspects of positive youth development.

Managed-care companies are stressing service results. An emerging force in the shift to a focus on outcomes is the growth of managed care, with its emphasis on results-oriented service delivery systems. Increasingly, managed-care companies are requiring nonprofit organizations that seek to be certified for payment to measure participant outcomes as part of the certification process. Affiliates of Catholic Charities USA and Family Service America, for example, are facing this issue in the counseling and home health care areas.

In some cases, managed-care companies are essentially dictating outcomes for programs, sometimes based on little more than intuition about what a desired outcome may be. At this point, there are no standard, managed-care outcomes for human services.

The emergence of managed care as a driver of outcome measurement is a major development that could have far-reaching effects on outcome measurement in the nonprofit sector. As yet, however, the implications of this development are receiving little discussion outside of the program areas directly affected.

Accrediting bodies are considering outcome-related criteria. In part as a response to the interests of managed-care companies, certifying and accrediting bodies are increasingly including standards for outcome measurement in their review criteria. For example:

The Accreditation Council on Services for People with Disabilities has published *The Outcome Based Performance Measures: A Procedures Manual* (1995). The manual lists specific outcomes for people with disabilities, suggests ways agencies seeking accreditation can assess these outcomes, and describes the independent quality-review process the Accreditation Council uses to confirm an agency's self-assessment.

The Council on Accreditation of Services for Families and Children's *Manual for Agency Accreditation* (1992) includes requirements that agencies collect data on program and client service quality and evaluate agency effectiveness, with client outcomes as a necessary component. The manual does not establish which outcomes should be tracked or provide data collection guidance.

Local agencies are operating effective outcome measurement systems. In addition to these national efforts, many local human service agencies—perhaps two to three thousand—have developed sound outcome monitoring approaches using a variety of internal and external resources. Although their number is small in comparison to the entire nonprofit human service sector, they represent a significant and growing segment of the field.

Lessons Learned in the Nonprofit Sector

All this activity has taught the field much about which approaches are productive and which practices impede success. Offered here are thirty useful lessons in five areas: the value of outcome measurement, agency implementation, the role of funders, effective uses of outcome findings in resource allocation, and limitations of outcome measurement.

Lessons About the Value of Outcome Measurement

1.   Outcome measurement benefits agencies in multiple ways—ways that counting outputs cannot. It helps them, for example, provide feedback and direction to staff, focus board members on policy and programmatic issues, identify training and technical assistance needs, pinpoint service units and participant groups that need attention, compare alternate service delivery strategies, identify partners for collaborations, allocate resources, recruit volunteers, attract customers, set targets for future performance, track program effectiveness over time, increase funding, and enhance their public image.

2.   Most programs benefit from simply discussing their intended outcomes. Staff often have varying views of what the program is trying to achieve, and getting everyone focused in the same direction can increase service effectiveness before data collection even begins.

3.   The most important reason for implementing outcome measurement is that it helps programs improve services. It can also increase accountability, guide managers in allocating resources, and help funders make better funding decisions, but its value in enhancing service effectiveness should be seen as primary.

Lessons About Effective Implementation by Agencies

4.   Outcome measurement is doable. Its nonexperimental design and basic data-analysis requirements make it manageable for even small, grassroots programs.

5.   Commitment at the top is essential. Otherwise, the task gets overcome by the other demands of program operation. Before they will commit to outcome measurement, however, agency directors and board presidents must see its value for their agencies.

6. Programs must identify their own outcomes, outcome indicators, and data collection procedures that are relevant and useful to their own efforts. Outcomes and indicators imposed by outsiders are unlikely to meet these criteria.

7. Creating a written logic model of program inputs, activities, outputs, and outcomes is a helpful way to think through the changes participants experience during and after the program and to check the logic of the if-then influences the program intends to set in motion.

8. Agencies should tap many perspectives when identifying program outcomes. Program volunteers, current and past participants (and perhaps family members), persons such as teachers and employers, and other agencies can point out important outcomes that do not occur to staff.

9. Outcome measurement does not always require new data collection efforts. Agencies often already compile data that reflect on outcomes.

10. Data collection and analysis may pose technical challenges that agencies do not have the in-house capacity to meet. The first time around, guidance on collection and analysis methods from a technical expert will often save time, offer reassurance, and improve results.

11. A trial run of the outcome measurement system is essential and will lead to changes in the system. The trial run must last long enough to encompass all key data collection points and must involve at least a representative group of program participants. Everyone should expect that the trial run will identify problems; that is its purpose.

12. Developing a sound outcome measurement system takes time—to plan, to try out, to adjust, and to implement. It easily could take an agency seven months or more of preparation before collecting any data, and it easily could take three to five years or more before the findings from a program's outcome measurement system actually reflect the program's effectiveness. Rushing the development process decreases the likelihood that the findings will be meaningful.

13. One useful approach to creating an outcome measurement system (Hatry, van Houten, Plantz, and Greenway, 1996) identifies eight steps grouped in three developmental phases: initial preparation (getting ready to begin, choosing outcomes to measure, specifying indicators for the outcomes, and preparing to collect data), a trial run (trying out data collection procedures and data analysis and reporting methods), and implementation (adjusting the outcome measurement system and using the findings).

14. Once implemented, the outcome measurement system must be monitored and improved continuously. Programs change and programs learn. The system must keep up.

Lessons About Useful Roles for Funders

15. Funders of nonprofit programs, including government agencies, national and local foundations, corporate philanthropic programs, and United Way organizations, will play a key role in the nonprofit sector's move to a focus

on outcomes. To be most constructive, funders should view their role as helping each program develop the outcome measurement approach that provides the most useful information for that program. To the extent that funders impose outcomes, measures, or timetables that do not align with agencies' efforts, they impede successful implementation.

16. Funders serve their own best interests by helping agencies develop capacity for outcome measurement. If agencies do not do well at outcome measurement, funders receive meaningless data or must acknowledge that they are supporting ineffective programs.

17. Building capacity requires much more than showing agencies how to complete forms. It involves hands-on, experiential training and ongoing technical assistance. Before engaging trainers or technical assistance providers, funders should ensure that they have applied experience in local nonprofit settings and are supportive of nonexperimental outcome monitoring approaches.

18. Local funders can collaborate with each other very effectively to support agency efforts. They can, for example, pool resources to underwrite training and technical assistance. They also can agree on outcome measurement terminology, methodology, and implementation timetables. Common application and reporting forms go even further in clarifying expectations and reducing the burden of paperwork on local agencies.

19. Funders can help agencies by providing an outside perspective on the reasonableness of agencies' outcome measurement plans and by working collaboratively to help improve the proposed approach. Funders should accept outcomes, indicators, and measurement methods established by relevant national organizations and accrediting bodies unless they fail to meet essential criteria.

20. As funders add outcome data as a reporting requirement, they should "walk the talk" of a focus on outcomes and drop existing reporting requirements that do not match this focus. If benefits for people are the critical emphasis, then some reports designed to monitor internal processes (for example, quarterly cash flow statements, detailed line-item budgets, salary information for specific staff, staffing structures, minutes of board meetings, and internal policy and procedure manuals) should be eliminated. This action also helps offset the added burden for agencies of collecting and reporting outcome data—a real benefit to agencies at a time when resources for the nonprofit sector are shrinking.

Lessons About Using Outcome Findings in Resource Allocation

21. Agency policymakers and funders who want outcomes to guide funding decisions need first to recognize the potential for harm. If done badly, linking outcomes to funding can shift resources from service delivery to measurement with no offsetting benefit to programs, penalize prevention and development programs and others with harder-to-measure outcomes, promote "creaming" (selecting participants who are more likely to succeed), inhibit innovation, punish risk-taking, and discourage interprogram cooperation.

22. Effective funding processes concentrate initially on ensuring that outcome measurement systems are sound. Wise fund allocators focus first on whether a program is making a good-faith effort at outcome measurement, not on the outcome findings themselves.

23. Once programs are sure they have specified the appropriate outcomes, fund allocators can consider whether those outcomes align with funding priorities. The issue of alignment is separate from that of program effectiveness and may be considered before outcome data are available. A danger in decisions regarding alignment, however, is that remediation programs may be favored over preventive or developmental programs, because at first glance outcomes of the latter do not appear to be linked to funding priorities. For example, if preventing teen pregnancy is a priority, the alignment of a program to prevent teen mothers from having repeat pregnancies is more readily apparent than the alignment of a program that seeks to engage twelve- to fifteen-year-olds in after-school programs to develop competencies and assertiveness skills. Over time, however, the second program may do more to address the priority.

24. Requiring program managers to set outcome targets before they have at least a year of baseline outcome data is counterproductive. Programs with no experience in outcome measurement generally have no basis for setting an appropriate target, and their targets will likely be little more than guesses. If actual performance falls below uninformed targets, there is a potential for unwarranted negative consequences.

25. Fund allocators do not yet have enough experience with outcome measurement to judge whether a particular level of achieved performance is good, bad, or in between. Arbitrary criterion levels are likely to be unrealistic and therefore not helpful.

26. Comparing seemingly similar programs to reward those with the best outcomes is tempting but misguided. Even seemingly similar programs have meaningful differences in mission, target audience, geographic location, staffing, service methodology, funding level, and many other descriptors that must be considered in assessing effectiveness. Fund allocators can use data from other programs to ask questions and probe why the outcome levels are different, but not to determine which program is better.

27. In judging outcome findings, the best comparison for a program is itself: Is the program improving? Is it learning from earlier outcome findings, making adjustments, and having better results?

28. Despite the hope of many fund allocators, outcome findings will not make the allocation decision easier. Decisions about where to direct resources will remain complex and value based, and funding decisions always will need to consider more than outcome performance. Factors such as target population, service delivery strategy, number served, outcomes intended, and program cost will continue to be important in deciding where to invest limited resources.

Lessons About Limitations of Outcome Measurement

29. There are many things outcome measurement does not do. It does not eliminate the need to monitor resources, activities, and outputs; tell a program whether it is measuring the right outcomes; explain why a program achieved a particular level of outcome; prove that the program caused the observed outcomes; show by itself what to do to improve the outcome; or answer the judgment question of whether the outcome is one in which resources should be invested.

30. Measuring and improving program-level outcomes does not, by itself, improve community-level outcomes. Except in rare instances, an individual program does not serve enough individuals to affect community-wide statistics, regardless of how successful the program is. In addition, community-level conditions are the result of a constellation of influences (such as economic conditions, environmental factors, demographic trends, public- and private-sector policies, cultural norms, and expectations) that are far beyond the scope of influence of individual human service programs.

Challenges for the Future

As the previous section shows, the nonprofit sector has learned many important lessons about outcome measurement. One more lesson is that there still is a lot to learn. Perhaps evaluators can help overcome some of the following seven key challenges.

Measuring harder-to-measure outcomes. Some programs face special challenges in measuring outcomes. These include programs whose participants are anonymous; those that provide very short-term assistance, such as emergency food or shelter; and those involved in prevention, development, public education, and advocacy and in providing support to other agencies. These programs need creative ideas for using existing records, third-party reports, trained observers, research-based milestones, secondary data, and other data sources and collection strategies. They also need measurable and meaningful approximations of their outcomes, which they can track while feasible measurement methods are developed.

Increasing useful input from research studies. Wider, more application-oriented communication of the results of experimental and quasi-experimental outcome studies, synthesized to their most actionable elements, would serve several purposes. It would provide research-based links between the initial or intermediate outcomes that programs are able to track, as well as the longer-term outcomes they cannot track but that are of interest to funders and policymakers. It also would help identify effective practices in human services, demonstrate alternative measurement approaches and tools, and add to the knowledge base regarding appropriate performance targets and benchmarks.

Sharing useful outcomes and indicators and successful tools and methods. Currently, most nonprofit agencies are working on outcome measurement in relative isolation, but it makes little sense for every program to start from scratch. Dictating common outcomes for programs dealing with similar issues is a counterproductive approach. However, establishing systems for sharing information about successful efforts and the context in which they were applied will save the field much time and expense, particularly benefiting agencies not supported by a national group. Such systems would also contribute to more rapid advancement in the state of the art.

Developing computer capacity to store, analyze, report, and track outcome data. Most agencies and funders have computers, typically used for word processing, but few have the software and skills needed to manage outcome data usefully. The field is in immediate need of easy-to-use models built on common, off-the-shelf software; guidance concerning key variables, database structure, and data manipulation requirements; and analysis and reporting examples specifically geared to outcome data management.

Guiding reviewers of outcome measurement plans in judging the appropriateness of proposed outcomes, indicators, and measures. Agency board members, funders' staff, and volunteers and other individuals will be reviewing outcome measurement plans. Often, reviewers have neither hands-on experience nor expertise in the programs whose plans they are reviewing. What criteria do they use to judge whether a proposed plan is sound? On what basis do they ask questions or offer suggestions? Resources to help reviewers offer input that is helpful, rather than distracting, would be of great value.

Establishing reasonable ranges for performance targets or benchmarks and identifying appropriate adjustments for different program and participant characteristics. For most program areas, there is insufficient information about what constitutes good performance. In a program working to move homeless families toward self-sufficiency, for example, suppose 20 percent of participating families are in independent, self-supported living situations within a year. Is this an abysmal failure or a tremendous success? A comparative figure would help program managers, as well as funders, evaluate the meaning of the finding. However, the adoption of targets must be done with great care. The same program in a different setting or serving a different population can reasonably have very different results. Identifying key variables that can be expected to relate to different levels of performance is an important safeguard against broad-brush application of criterion levels.

Creating methodologies for aligning program-level outcomes with broader efforts to create community-level change. Measuring program outcomes has value as an end in itself. However, program outcomes also can contribute to, and should be aligned with, broader efforts to effect community-level change. Such change requires a spectrum of activities, including advocating with key players, establishing multipartner collaborations, supporting volunteer initiatives, influencing public- and private-sector policies, and leveraging funders' money. Effective theories of change (Connell and Kubisch, in press) can tie these elements and the outcomes of individual programs into a coordinated whole with the scope needed to affect community issues.

Conclusion

Nonprofit agencies often ask if outcome measurement is just a fad that, if ignored long enough, will go away. The consensus of the field is a resounding "No." As are earlier aspects of performance measurement that built on each other to strengthen the management and delivery of nonprofit services, the careful measurement of outcomes is an essential building block that informs us in new and necessary ways about how to improve programs. It is not the last brick to be added, nor has it developed as far as it can and will. However, outcome measurement is here to stay, and the nonprofit sector and the individuals it serves will be better for it.

References

Accreditation Council on Services for People with Disabilities. *The Outcome Based Performance Measures: A Procedures Manual.* Towson, Md.: The Accreditation Council on Services for People with Disabilities, 1995.

Boy Scouts of America. *Scouting's Positive Impact on the Community: A Resource for Measuring Program Outcomes.* Irving, Tex.: Boy Scouts of America, 1996.

Brown, S., and Conn, M. Girl Scouts: *Who We Are, What We Think.* New York: Girl Scouts of America, 1990.

Child Welfare League of America. *The Odyssey Project: A Descriptive and Prospective Study of Children in Residential Treatment, Group Homes, and Therapeutic Foster Care.* Washington, D.C.: Child Welfare League of America, 1995.

Connell, J. P., and Kubisch, A. C. "Applying a Theory of Change Approach to the Evaluation of Comprehensive Community Initiatives: Progress, Prospects and Problems." In *New Approaches to Evaluating Community Initiatives: Concepts, Methods, and Context.* Washington, D.C.: The Aspen Institute, in press.

Council on Accreditation of Services for Families and Children. *Manual for Agency Accreditation.* New York: Council on Accreditation of Services for Families and Children, 1992.

Elkin, R., and Molitor, M. *Management Indicators in Nonprofit Organizations: Guidelines to Selection and Implementation.* Baltimore: University of Maryland, School of Social Work and Community Planning, 1984.

Frederick, J., and Nicholson, H. *Assess for Success.* Indianapolis: Girls Incorporated, 1991.

Goodwill Industries International. *Program Evaluation: Guidelines for Development and Implementation.* Bethesda, Md.: Goodwill Industries International, 1994.

Hatry, H., van Houten, T., Plantz, M. C., and Greenway, M. T. *Measuring Program Outcomes: A Practical Approach.* Alexandria, Va.: United Way of America, 1996.

Hodgkinson, V., and Weitzman, M. S. *Nonprofit Almanac 1996–1997: Dimensions of the Independent Sector.* San Francisco: Jossey-Bass, 1996.

Jacobs, L., Nicholson, H., Plotch, A., and Weiss, F. *It's My Party: Girls Choose to be Substance Free.* Indianapolis: Girls Incorporated, 1993.

National Health Council and National Assembly for Social Policy and Development. *Standards of Accounting and Financial Reporting for Voluntary Health and Welfare Organizations.* New York: National Health Council and National Assembly for Social Policy and Development, 1964.

Nicholson, H., Postrada, L., and Weiss, F. *Truth, Trust and Technology: New Research on Preventing Adolescent Pregnancy.* Indianapolis: Girls Incorporated, 1991.

Peterson, D. *An Evaluation of an Elementary School Based Intergenerational Linkages Program: Mentoring for Academic Enrichment.* Philadelphia: Big Brothers Big Sisters of America, 1994.

Taylor, M. E., and Sumariwalla, R. D. "Evaluating Nonprofit Effectiveness: Overcoming the Barriers." In D. R. Young, V. A. Hodgkinson, R. M. Hollister, and Associates, *Governing, Leading, and Managing Nonprofit Organizations: New Insights from Research and Practice.* San Francisco: Jossey-Bass, 1993.

Tierney, J., Grossman, J. and Resch, N. *Making a Difference: An Impact Study of Big Brothers Big Sisters.* Philadelphia: Public/Private Ventures, 1995.

United Way of America. *Accounting and Financial Reporting: A Guide for United Ways and Not-for-Profit Human Service Organizations.* Alexandria, Va.: United Way of America, 1974.

United Way of America. *UWASIS II: A Taxonomy of Social Goals & Human Service Programs.* Alexandria, Va.: United Way of America, 1976.

MARGARET C. PLANTZ *is director of evaluation for United Way of America.*

MARTHA TAYLOR GREENWAY *is senior director, Effective Practices and Measuring Impact, United Way of America.*

MICHAEL HENDRICKS *is an Oregon-based independent consultant specializing in program planning, performance monitoring and evaluation, organizational development, and technical assistance and training.*

Recent events that have encouraged performance measurement in local governments and local private nonprofit organizations are described in this chapter. The author discusses some obstacles managers face in measuring outcomes at the local level, and he offers successful uses of outcomes reporting to address citizen concerns.

Where the Rubber Meets the Road: Performance Measurement for State and Local Public Agencies

Harry P. Hatry

As the old saying goes, it is where "the rubber meets the road" that counts. For public services, this place is at the direct service delivery level—where trash is collected, tickets are issued, and taxes are paid. Unfortunately, state and local governments have considerably fewer resources for evaluation and performance measurement than do federal agencies. Nevertheless, state and local agencies need the tools of evaluation and performance measurement for tracking progress and for achieving accountability to the public. This need will continue to grow, especially as current devolutionary trends continue and taxpayers expect more for less.

This chapter first addresses recent major performance measurement events. Then it discusses emerging new directions and obstacles to the use of measurement information. It concludes with a discussion of the relationship of performance measurement to program evaluation.

Recent Events

In recent years, a number of state and local governments have begun moving toward outcome-based performance measurement. Some important events have been the following:

The author thanks Ron Carlee of the Department of Human Services of Arlington County, Va., for his very helpful suggestions for this chapter.

The Total Quality Management movement, beginning in the 1980s in state and local governments in the United States, has encouraged an explicit focus on customers and feedback from customers on services. Many state and local legislators are business people; they are often familiar with customer surveys.

The Governmental Accounting Standards Board (GASB), beginning in the early 1990s, has pressed for experimentation on what it calls "service efforts and accomplishments" reporting by state and local governments (Governmental Accounting Standards Board, 1990, 1994). GASB is a private nonprofit organization that develops accounting standards for state and local governments to use as a basis for external reporting. The service efforts and accomplishments movement's primary new thrust is on reporting outcomes (accomplishments). This effort has encouraged a number of governments to begin outcomes reporting. For example, since 1991, the city of Portland, Oregon, through its audit office, has been issuing a document called "Service Efforts and Accomplishments: Annual Report on City Government and Performance." The city auditor collects information from individual agencies and through an annual mail survey of approximately ten thousand randomly selected households. This survey asks households for ratings of a number of public services.

At the beginning of the 1990s, a number of state legislatures, led by Oregon and Texas, introduced annual requirements for performance measurement by state agencies. In Texas, performance indicators have been included in the state legislature's annual appropriations bill. Oregon's legislatively generated benchmark effort has been the progenitor of a number of subsequent public-sector efforts by other state and local governments, including the states of Minnesota and Florida. These efforts have identified outcome-oriented indicators for broad, statewide objectives, somewhat resembling the social indicator movement of the 1970s. (State agencies have had problems attempting to introduce outcome measurements that directly relate to these broad state goals.)

The use of regular (for example, annual) customer surveys has been expanding considerably. Efforts have included annual random samples of households covering a range of services (such as those being done by Portland, Oregon, and Prince William County, Virginia) and surveys by individual agencies of their own clients on one or only a few services (such as those being done by the Ramsey County, Minnesota, Department of Human Services).

The performance management process of Sunnyvale, California, begun in the 1980s, if not the 1970s, gained notoriety when one of its ex-mayors became a key staff member on the Senate Government Affairs Committee. He helped develop the Government Performance and Results Act of 1993, which likely will have major implications in the long run for states and local governments. The Act (Public Law 103-62, Aug. 3, 1993) requires each federal program to identify indicators of outcome for major programs, to provide targets at the beginning of each fiscal year for each indicator, and to report on the actual values for each outcome indicator within six months after the end of the fiscal year. Sunnyvale's initial focus was primarily on indicators of productivity (indices of the relationship of the amount of output to the amount of resources applied). In recent years, however, Sunnyvale has added outcomes to its data collection efforts. Sunnyvale has gone quite far in imbuing its managers with a focus on results in their management and budgeting activities.

Many other local governments have introduced annual requirements for performance information with an explicit requirement for outcome data. These include such varied local governments as Charlotte, North Carolina, and New York City (whose sanitation department has been using photographic rating scales for many years to track the cleanliness of streets in each district throughout the city, using that data as a basis for allocating its street cleaning crews).

The greatly improved, and extremely more powerful and quick, data processing hardware and software of the late 1980s and 1990s has greatly enhanced the practicality of regular outcome measurement. This technology has provided the ability to provide quick response time inexpensively, so that public managers and their personnel can receive feedback on outcome data within a few weeks, even days, after the period for which data have been reported. The technology also enables managers and others to readily obtain outcome information broken out in many different ways, such as by different categories of customers.

Internationally, countries such as Australia, New Zealand, and Great Britain have moved heavily into performance measurement. The World Bank has stepped up its interest in evaluation, including regular tracking of performance information. Some World Bank staff have been encouraging and assisting developing countries to undertake service delivery surveys that use sample surveys of citizens to assess the quality of the services they receive from their governments. This endeavor is an ongoing program of the World Bank's Economic Development Institute. Such international efforts tend to reinforce each other. For example, developments such as New Zealand and Australia giving more flexibility and more authority to agencies in return for more accountability on what the agencies produce, have begun to increase similar interest in the U.S. public sector.

Some New Directions

The following are some of the emerging directions that appear likely to encourage performance measurement at state and local government levels even further, at least over the next few years:

- Performance-based partnerships
- Greatly expanded use of customer feedback approaches, such as customer surveys
- Much greater use of outcome-based performance contracts
- Much greater involvement of the nongovernmental sector in performance measurement
- Much greater reporting to citizens on outcome information
- New accountability paradigms

Each of these is discussed in the next section.

Performance Partnerships. A major new development is the recognition by public agencies, at all levels, that outcomes are seldom caused solely by a single public-sector agency. The agency may not even be a major influence. Other public agencies and private sector elements usually have important roles in producing desired outcomes.

The term *performance partnerships* has begun to be used, especially by federal and state governments. Such partnership should entail joint and equal participation by all partners in selecting the outcomes sought, the associated outcome indicators, the associated data collection procedures to be used to track the progress of the partnership, and time-phased targets for each indicator. This implies a more equal partnership than the federal government appears to have been willing to permit in the past. The partners should also agree on each partner's roles and responsibilities in producing the outcomes.

The state of Oregon and its local governments have been leaders in the concept of performance partnerships. The Oregon Progress Board (in Salem), a product of the state legislature and partnered with the governor, began to identify outcome indicators and the joint roles of the state, cities, counties, federal government, school districts, and the private sector (including businesses, churches, and families). For example, working to reduce the number of teenage pregnancies, the Progress Board identified each of the following as having important roles: state agencies, including health, education, and public welfare agencies; county and city agencies; school districts; churches; and parents. It is attempting to work with them on strategies to reduce teenage pregnancy. At the local level, Portland and Multnomah County established a joint Progress Board of their own, identifying a set of outcome indicators, compatible with the state's benchmark indicators but more specific to local services.

An example of such partnerships is the Jobs Training Partnership Act (JTPA), which has involved federal, state, and local agencies in developing a small set of performance indicators (such as the percentage of clients who are employed thirteen weeks after completion of the local program, and their average earnings at that time). The data are developed locally and provided to the U.S. Department of Labor (DOL). DOL provides data back to the states. State governments are responsible for overseeing their own JTPA programs and for using federal funds as rewards for local programs that do well on the indicators, or as means of providing assistance or sanctions to those that have not met their targets. DOL has developed a process for providing national targets, primarily based on past average performance. DOL recommends but does not require that local targets be adjusted for selected conditions, such as economic factors, that are likely to affect the ability of local programs to place clients in jobs.

Use of Customer Surveys. An important technical development sweeping the country at all three levels of government, especially federal and local, is the increased use of regular customer surveys to assess the quality and outcomes of public services. President Clinton's 1993 executive order "Setting Customer Service Standards" (Executive Order #12862, Sept. 11, 1993) requires such surveys of many federal programs.

Local governments have also begun to use regular surveys to obtain customers' evaluations and probably did so earlier than the federal government. For example, Portland and Prince William County have been undertaking annual household surveys to obtain evaluative feedback. As noted earlier, the auditor's office of Portland has undertaken an annual mail survey of approximately ten thousand households starting in 1991. The results of these surveys are reported in its annual "Service Efforts and Accomplishments" reports. These surveys ask citizens to evaluate a number of government services. The office has been amazingly successful in achieving, through multiple mailings, response rates of 42 to 53 percent, with an average of close to 50 percent. In some years the office also supplements the mail survey with telephone interviews with small samples of nonrespondents to compare the results; so far, differences have not been major.

Prince William County has undertaken annual telephone surveys of approximately eight hundred households since 1993. Another example is Minnesota's Department of Trade and Economic Development. It has undertaken periodic surveys of its business customers about such services as its small business assistance and export promotion programs.

Many other city and county governments have begun to undertake similar surveys. Dayton, Ohio, was an early leader in this effort, taking annual surveys, beginning in the 1970s, of random samples of its citizens to obtain citizen rating of a number of city services.

In addition, individual agencies have begun to undertake regular surveys of their own clients. These agencies have the mailing addresses and telephone numbers of their customers. Their surveys are usually done by mail, but sometimes by phone, to make regular surveys practical. Obtaining decent response rates (50 percent or more) is a challenge but seems achievable when a service agency requests feedback from its customers.

The term *customer satisfaction survey* has sometimes been used for such surveys. If surveys ask only about overall satisfaction with services, they might not have very much value, as some critics have pointed out. However, surveys often can and should go well beyond merely asking about overall customer satisfaction. They can also obtain ratings of specific service characteristics and gather various factual data such as employment rates; days lost to health problems; crime victimization; and frequency of use of parks, libraries, and public transit. Such information can be very useful to agency managers for tracking results and identifying service problem areas.

This emerging activity has both practical and technical problems. Surveys cost money, a scarce commodity for most state and local agencies. Surveys have to be done soundly, including proper selection of the sample, design of the questionnaires, and handling of the responses, to obtain adequate response rates and provide quality information. Regular customer surveys are still fairly new to most state and local governments. Many governments have long histories of sponsoring surveys, but not regular surveys on quality and outcome-based surveys. Public agencies usually have used contractors for surveys of samples of households. For surveys of an agency's own clients by mail (mail often being the only practical option), agencies are faced both with resource limitations and technical accuracy questions.

Each government needs to consider what form of quality control should be exercised over its surveys. Some central oversight is probably needed, perhaps by a small, central analytical office that provides quality control over the survey work of the government's agencies, or by an internal audit group.

Customer surveys provide part of the running outcome scores of the progress of these agencies. In general, however, that information does not indicate the extent to which the programs have caused the outcomes. There is a partial exception. Survey questionnaires can be included that ask customers for their perceptions as to "the extent to which the agency's service contributed to the outcomes." Such questions were used by the Family Service Association of America for several years in its regular surveys (now discontinued) for its local member family services organizations of customers of family counseling programs (Beck and Jones, 1980). Minnesota used similar questions in its export promotion program surveys of assisted businesses (Fink and Kosecoff, 1985; Naumann and Giel, 1995).

Performance Contracting. A major emerging application of outcome measurement is *performance contracting*. Performance contracting is contracting for services in which the contracts identify specific performance indicators, especially outcome indicators. The contracts usually include specific numerical targets to be accomplished for each outcome indicator identified in the contract. Sometimes, but not always, the contractor's compensation is directly linked to achievement of the contract targets. For example, Wisconsin's Division of Vocational Rehabilitation included such provisions in some of its contracts with private nonprofit agencies that provided employment services. These contracts based contractor compensation solely on the number of clients that the private agency placed for a minimum amount of time and for a wage of at least a specified amount (Hatry and Durman, 1985). Drug treatment contractors have also been compensated, at least in part, in relation to their ability to provide evidence that a certain number of clients had abstained from drug use for a specific length of time.

Maine and Arkansas have passed legislation that requires performance contracts in their human service programs. These states have been struggling to implement these provisions in a reasonably valid manner.

Performance contracting presents the following technical evaluation challenges:

The contracting government needs to establish a reasonably valid and reliable tracking system for each of the indicators included in the contract. It also needs to monitor the quality of the information provided. The government needs to determine the extent to which contractors provide the basic data (subject to government audit) versus the government agency itself. Developing contract provisions that are fair to both the public and the contractors is a major challenge.

Performance contracts, and the related contractor compensation, implicitly assume that contractors will be rewarded (or penalized) regardless of whether or not the outcome success was actually caused by the contractor. State and local governments using performance contracting seldom, if ever, have undertaken in-depth evaluations to assess the extent to which the contractors contributed to the outcomes identified. As discussed in this chapter, in the section, "New Accountability Paradigm," practical problems in undertaking regular in-depth, causality-based program evaluation probably make in-depth evaluations infeasible as an ongoing part of performance contracting.

Outcome-based contracting places the burden on the contracting organization to develop a capacity to properly monitor contractors' achievements. This burden is new to government agencies. It is yet to be seen how effective this approach will be. Performance contracting, however, appears to have the potential to be an appropriate approach to improving the quality of services.

Use by Private Nonprofit Organizations of Performance Measurement. Local private nonprofit organizations have also, in recent years, begun to introduce performance measurement focused on outcomes. Many private human service delivery organizations are supported at least partially by state and local agencies. To the extent those private agencies successfully implement outcome-based performance measurement, this should greatly ease the outcome measurement burden on their sponsoring organizations. The Family Services Association of America effort mentioned earlier was a forerunner of this effort.

More recently, United Way organizations, as well as a number of other national private nonprofit organizations, have begun to be pressed by their donors for information as to what their donated funds are achieving, not just how the dollars are being spent. This pressure led in 1996 to a major effort on outcome monitoring by United Way of America. It developed a training program and training manuals on outcome measurement for private nonprofit service delivery agencies (United Way of America, 1996a, 1996b). United Way chapters in Minneapolis, Milwaukee, New Orleans, Rochester, and Toronto have been among the leaders. A growing number of local United Ways have begun requiring grant recipients to provide data on service outcomes. The data collection procedures being emphasized have been to use surveys of clients to obtain information on the extent of improvement in their situations since coming in for services and their satisfaction with the services.

This, in some ways, is a remarkable development. Many local private nonprofit programs are quite small and without personnel experienced in quantitative techniques and program evaluation. The key technical question is whether such agencies can provide outcome data of adequate quality. Organizations such as local United Ways will need to provide good technical assistance (perhaps through local universities and volunteer specialists) to the service delivery agencies. The availability of inexpensive computers and software makes substantial progress possible.

Another potentially remarkable private sector development is the interest by accreditation organizations in including service results, or at least evidence that a tangible program performance measurement effort is under way, in their accreditation criteria. An early, perhaps premature, effort at this was undertaken by the Commission on Accreditation of Rehabilitative Facilities in the late 1970s and early 1980s (Commission on Accreditation of Rehabilitative Facilities, 1977).

In January 1997, the Joint Commission on Accreditation of Health Care Organizations announced that it is beginning to consider the outcomes of a facility's patients, and not just the quality of its staff and equipment, when deciding which hospital to approve (Joint Commission on Accreditation of Health Care Organizations, 1997).

The National Accreditation Council for Agencies Serving the Blind and Visually Handicapped started a major effort in 1997 to encourage accredited agencies to develop consistent, agreed-upon methods of collecting and analyzing outcomes to permit valid comparisons of program effectiveness between organizations in different settings (National Accreditation Council for Agencies Serving the Blind, 1997). Other national accreditation organizations seem likely to move in this direction in the future, such as those for public safety (police, fire, and corrections).

Public Reporting of Outcome Information. How many readers of this journal have, in the past year (or ever) received data (that they did not seek to obtain for themselves) from their local, state, or federal governments on the outcomes of a service? The history is that few government agencies have actually reported on a regular basis to the public on service outcomes. However, in recent years, some data have begun to be regularly reported to the public, such as number of crimes reported, school test score results, air pollution levels, and some health data.

A small number of governments have provided outcome information in public reports on a regular, annual basis. One of the oldest reports is that issued annually by New York City. The city has issued a Mayor's Management Report for many years and during the administrations of many different mayors. Though much of its content has been output information, some outcome data have been included, such as ratings of street cleanliness for various parts of the city. The Province of Alberta, Canada, began issuing in 1994 an annual report entitled "Measuring Up" that primarily provides outcome data (including some data obtained from sample customer surveys). Portland, Oregon, and Prince William County, Virginia, have been producing annual reports called "Service Efforts and Accomplishments" in recent years. Each report contains a substantial number of outcome indicators, including some whose data are obtained through customer surveys.

This type of external reporting of outcome information has been greatly encouraged by the Governmental Accounting Standards Board (GASB), the private nonprofit organization that has traditionally provided recommendations to state and local governments as to their financial accounting and reporting processes. Beginning about 1990, GASB began to encourage what it calls "service efforts and accomplishments" external reporting to elected officials and citizens. Outcome reporting is the major new element covered by this movement. GASB has called for state and local governments to experiment with such reporting but has not yet recommended that such reporting be mandated by state and local legislative bodies (Governmental Accounting Standards Board, 1990, 1994)

The State of Florida recently issued its first benchmarks report (*The Florida Benchmarks Report,* 1996). It uses a framework similar to that of the Oregon Benchmark biennial reports of the Oregon Progress Board and the Minnesota Milestones biennial reports. These reports, however, all contain statewide quality-of-life indicators for the states, rather than focusing on the outcomes of particular state agency programs.

New Accountability Paradigm. The concept of government accountability in past decades has focused on accountability for complying with laws, including the proper use of funds so that public resources are used for legal purposes. An additional focus has been on accountability for results. As noted elsewhere in this chapter, performance measurement, by itself, seldom indicates why the outcomes are the way they are. Without more in-depth evaluation, the "whys" are not likely to be clear. Once government agencies focus on outcomes, elected officials, the media, and the public need to recognize that the government agency is only one of many factors that are likely to affect outcomes. Many other organizations, citizens, and external factors can affect those outcomes.

Unfortunately, many people involved with performance measurement continue to believe that government agencies fully control and, thus, are fully accountable for outcomes. The implication is that if the outcomes are not met, the public agency is liable; if the actual outcomes are better than the outcome targets, the agency is responsible. This is an overly simplistic notion that can have disturbing implications, such as in attempts to link pay to performance, and blaming agency managers before considering the "whys." The evaluation community, including performance measurement personnel, needs to continually remind appointed government officials, elected officials, the media, and the public that accountability for outcomes is almost always shared.

Governments can face this complexity directly and attempt to assess causes and the extent to which the program contributed to the outcomes. This, however, is quite difficult, even with sophisticated program evaluations—and is expensive. Probably the most sensible approach, at least for the near future, is for all parties to recognize explicitly that public agencies have only partial control, and therefore, only partial accountability. This is not likely to satisfy many who want to hold government agencies fully accountable.

Obstacles to Effective Use of Outcome Information

Ultimately, the major purpose of regular outcome measurement should be to focus government personnel at all levels (from first-line employees to the chief executive and legislators) on the continual attempt to improve results. Thus far, performance measurement has been primarily used to respond to requirements imposed by the legislative body or officials of the executive branch. Evidence of the use of outcome data to improve programs is still lacking in most cases.

Major obstacles to effective use of outcome information include the following:

• Many public agencies have considerable difficulty developing outcome information. You cannot use what you do not have.

• Outcome data that are provided are usually too highly aggregated to be meaningful for lower-level personnel. Citywide or statewide data provide a summary of the outcomes but hide much information as to how the program is working for different categories of customers and for different key service characteristics. Program evaluation personnel routinely break out their data on outcomes by such characteristics. This, however, is not nearly as common in performance measurement in the public sector. For many programs it is clearly desirable to distinguish outcomes for various age groups, persons in different geographical parts of the agencies' jurisdiction, gender, ethnic or racial groups, income category, household size and composition, whether families own or rent their homes, educational level, and so on. In addition, outcome data becomes much more useful if segmented by the particular office or facility, such as an individual fire station, specific park, specific library, sanitation district, or social service office.

• Data reporting is often too infrequent. For managers to make full use of outcome information, they need to receive feedback on outcome relatively frequently so that they can make early adjustments and, in later reports, determine whether those adjustments have been accompanied by outcome improvements. Quarterly reporting for managers is fairly common throughout U.S. governments but is not as common for outcome information.

For example, surveys of citizens are typically done once a year, at most. For operational purposes, why not split the survey budget into quarters and administer the questionnaire to a fourth of the sample each quarter? This would cost somewhat more and would provide less precision in each quarter's findings (though the precision would improve as the data from later quarters were added) but would provide managers with much more timely and seasonal information. Some outcomes are not likely to change that quickly; however, the selection of questions in each quarter's survey can take that into consideration. Note that the findings of a survey of 1,000 customers undertaken at one time during the year should not be expected to be the same as the cumulative outcome from four quarterly surveys of 250 customers each. The combined data using quarterly subsamples may, in fact, be more meaningful to public managers than an annual snapshot of information, because the combined data may capture a better perspective on performance throughout the year.

• The state of the art in outcome measurement is limited. For example, it is very difficult to measure prevention of crimes, fires, child abuse, and so on. Therefore, agencies measure nonprevention as a substitute. They measure the number of crimes, fires, or cases of child abuse that are reported—not the number prevented. Another example is the following: How do you measure the outcomes of hotlines in which callers are anonymous, thereby preventing follow-ups of callers to assess the helpfulness of the hotline?

• The relationships between resources (cost and number of employees) and outcomes is seldom known, nor is it likely to be well known even under the best conditions. The most-discussed use for outcome data is for its use in budgeting. However, it is optimistic to believe that officials will be able to make good predictions of outcomes that would result from particular levels of budgets. It is one thing to systematically measure past performance; it is another to make predictions about future outcomes. How many additional resources are needed to bring customer satisfaction rates or customer employment up five percentage points over the next year? Such predictions require much more than retrospective program evaluation and outcome measurement. Predictions involve prospective program analysis, something very seldom done in a systematic way by state and local (or federal) agencies. This is an inherent problem for which few solutions may be available in the foreseeable future.

• Managers have little experience or training in how to use performance information, especially outcome information, to help improve their programs. Although one would think that this use would be instinctive to many managers, most are under considerable daily pressures to run their operations and to respond to immediate demands on their time. Help is needed to assist them to examine regularly obtained outcome data and, with their staffs, to identify which outcomes are less than desired, develop actions to strengthen those areas, and, later, look at future outcome reports to determine whether those actions have achieved what was hoped for—to help decide whether actions taken should be continued, expanded, or deleted and other actions tried instead.

• Performance measurement costs money and resources, as do in-depth program evaluations. Over the long run, performance measurement (and program evaluation in general) needs to provide evidence that the value of data collection is worth the cost.

Relationship of Performance Measurement to Program Evaluation

Performance measurement can be considered part of program evaluation. *Performance measurement* refers to the regular (usually annual) reporting of performance information, especially outcome information, for the programs of an agency. Outcome measurement focuses on the part of program evaluation that deals with estimating program outcomes but does not attempt to identify the extent to which the program caused the outcomes. In-depth program evaluations tend to be expensive and require special capabilities and attention. They therefore can only be used on some programs, and only infrequently. Performance measurement can cover a wide range of a government's or agency's programs—and be done on an ongoing basis.

Here are some further points on the relationship:

• In-depth program evaluations in the United States tend to be done by organizations outside government, such as contractors and universities. Performance measurement is normally done by agencies themselves (although certain data collection elements such as customer surveys may be contracted).

• A considerable amount of what is called program evaluation by state and local governments (at least by those evaluations that are not funded by the federal government) more closely resembles performance measurement than in-depth program evaluation. Much of the work that is labeled program evaluation by state and local governments is done by legislative evaluation or auditing organizations, not by the executive branch. These studies are usually after-the-fact assessments that focus on seeking data on outcomes without much explicit attention to the causality issue.

• A relatively small number of state and local governments have offices responsible for what is labeled *evaluation*. Much of what they seem to do is after-the-fact outcome measurement work. An example of the more advanced local evaluation work is that done by the Office of Research and Evaluation of the Ramsey County, Minnesota, Human Services Department. With its limited resources, it primarily does after-the-fact data collection and analysis. However, on occasion, the office has undertaken more sophisticated studies. For example, in 1995, the office identified a sample of eighty-five cases where the program office had made risk assessments for child protection service children when the case was opened and also at discharge. The office compared the level of risk at discharge to that at intake and reported on the changes (Ramsey County Office of Research and Evaluation, 1996). Such analysis is not usually done as part of performance measurement. However, this type of analysis still falls short of being in-depth, causality-based evaluation; it is still not known whether the outcomes were caused by the department's services or by other factors.

• Outcome measurement can be a substantial aid to in-depth program evaluation. If an agency has been collecting outcome data over time for its programs, undertaking in-depth evaluations will be easier. The evaluators can use the outcome data that the agency is collecting and apply more of its evaluation resources to other aspects of the evaluation. A problem, however, is that many agencies (at all levels of government) tend to collect outcome data primarily in aggregate. Often, public agencies do not also provide breakouts of the outcome data by such important characteristics as age, gender, geographical location, race or ethnicity, and educational level. Such information is often critical to identifying what is happening and where. As the performance measurement field becomes more mature, it seems inevitable that outcome information will also commonly be broken out by such characteristics. Such information makes the outcome information much more useful for program evaluations.

It is not often recognized that if an agency collects outcome data on an ongoing basis, randomized, controlled experiments are more feasible for some types of interventions. For example, if a human service program director wants to try a new procedure, the program could randomly assign a sample of customers to the new procedure and then separately track the random assignees and those that continued under the old program. Then, the program could use the regularly collected outcome data for each group of customers. Of course, other conditions for experiments need to be present, such as the ability to keep control of the experiment over the experimental period.

Similarly, outcome information will become considerably more useful if it is linked to accurate data on the amount of resources (dollars and staff) applied and to the physical outputs produced by the agency's programs. The performance measurement process should be constructed to provide information on the amount of dollars and staff time used to assist particular categories of customers, and on how many people were served by the program. The process should link such information to the associated outcomes. Currently, this is not usually done by state and local agencies. Improved cost accounting systems, as well as better outcome measurement procedures, will be needed by most governments.

Overall, it appears that performance measurement, especially that which is outcome-based, should be a substantial plus for program evaluators. It should lead to questioning by agency and external officials as to why outcomes are the way they are and encourage more in-depth program evaluations. It should help evaluators attempting to do in-depth evaluations by providing valuable outcome data that they would otherwise have to collect or that could not be obtained by other means (such as customer feedback obtained before the intervention was implemented).

Performance measurement should not be looked on as a substitute for in-depth evaluations but should be considered as complementary to them.

Conclusion

State and local agencies are moving toward outcome-based performance measurement, though at a slow pace. With limited technical resources to help, both in developing and using the outcome data, these agencies are somewhat handicapped. Nevertheless, it is important that they be encouraged to collect, analyze, and report reliable, valid data on outcomes as an aid to achieving better accountability, better resource allocation, and program improvement.

References

Beck, D. F., and Jones, M. A. *How to Conduct a Client Follow-up Study*. New York: Family Service Association of America, 1980.

Commission on Accreditation of Rehabilitative Facilities. *Program Evaluation in Vocational Rehabilitative Facilities*. Chicago: Commission on Accreditation of Rehabilitative Facilities, 1977.

Fink, A., and Kosecoff, J. *How to Conduct Surveys*. Thousand Oaks, Calif.: Sage, 1985.

The Florida Benchmarks Report. Tallahassee, Fla.: Florida Commission on Government Accountability to the People, Executive Office of the Governor, 1996.

Governmental Accounting Standards Board. *Service Efforts and Accomplishments Reporting: Its Time Has Come—An Overview*. Norwalk, Conn.: Governmental Accounting Standards Board, 1990.

Governmental Accounting Standards Board. *Concepts Statement Number 2: On Concepts Related to Service Efforts and Accomplishments Reporting*. Norwalk, Conn.: Governmental Accounting Standards Board, 1994.

Hatry, H., and Durman, E. *Issues in Competitive Contracting for Social Service*. Reston, Va.: The National Institute of Governmental Purchasing, 1985.

Joint Commission on Accreditation of Health Care Organizations. *Request for Indicators*. Oakbrook Terrace, Ill.: Joint Commission on Accreditation of Health Care Organizations, 1997.

National Accreditation Council for Agencies Serving the Blind and Visually Handicapped. *Outcomes Achieved by Consumers with Vision Loss Served by Specialized and General State VR Agencies*. New York: National Accreditation Council for Agencies Serving the Blind and Visually Handicapped, 1997.

Naumann, E., and Giel, K. *Customer Satisfaction Measurement and Management*. Cincinnati, Ohio: Thomson Executive Press, 1995.

Ramsey County Office of Research and Evaluation. *Community Human Services 1995 Program Evaluation Report*. St. Paul, Minn.: Ramsey County Office of Research and Evaluation, 1996.

United Way of America. *Measuring Program Outcomes: A Practical Approach*. Alexandria, Va.: United Way of America, 1996a.

United Way of America. *Focusing on Program Outcomes: A Guide for United Ways*. Alexandria, Va.: United Way of America, 1996b.

HARRY P. HATRY is director of state and local programs at The Urban Institute, Washington, D.C.

The challenges that face governments in developing performance-based budgeting systems are described in this chapter. Performance-based budgeting is placed in the context of past and current performance-based management reforms.

Using Performance Measures for Budgeting: A New Beat, or Is It the Same Old Tune?

Philip G. Joyce

> The field of administration is a field of business. It is removed from the hurry and strife of politics. . . . It is the object of administrative study to discover first, what government can properly do, and, secondly, how it can do these proper things with the utmost possible efficiency and the least possible cost either in money or in energy.
> Woodrow Wilson, 1887

> This performance review is not about politics. . . . We want to make improving the way government does business a permanent part of the way government works, regardless of which party is in power.
> National Performance Review, 1993.

The improvement of public administration has been a central concern of political and administrative reformers for well over one hundred years. The "reinventing government" movement, which has as one of its centerpieces an effort to increase the development and use of measures of government performance, is the latest manifestation of this desire. A central component of this new administrative orthodoxy involves using performance measures to fundamentally change the decision processes of government, including those involving resource allocation. The reformers, in short, want a system in which funds are allocated according to the results that are achieved by public programs, rather than being based primarily on the analysis of inputs—the dollars that flow from the program (Osborne and Gaebler, 1992; Gore, 1993b).

Although no one would want to seriously argue in opposition to such a results focus, it is particularly useful to review the assumptions implicit in the effort in the context of the intellectual history and practice of public administration. Do these assumptions embrace discredited ideas concerning the relationship between and among political leaders and the bureaucracy? Are these current reforms just a repeat of those that have been tried and failed in the past? If so, we can conclude that claims to reinvent government stand on shaky ground. If, on the other hand, there is something fundamentally different about either the reforms themselves or the environment in which they operate, the results could be fundamentally different from those of past reforms, which always seemed to deliver much less than promised.

With the foregoing in mind, this chapter will make three points:

The current efforts to expand the use of performance information for budgeting in the United States are being driven by efforts taking place in other countries, and are manifesting themselves in spotty (but often impressive) efforts in state and local governments and legislatively induced initiatives in the federal government.

If we place these current efforts in historical context, it suggests that caution is warranted, specifically concerning the potential for a reinvention of budgeting. Three particular challenges stand out—involving goal clarity, measurement, and applying measures to budget decisions—that face those who would seek to make government resource allocation decisions more performance-based.

The current state of performance-based budgeting in the United States suggests impressive but embryonic efforts to develop better performance measures at all levels of government, but no significant use of performance information in the resource allocation process.

The Rebirth of Performance-Based Budgeting

The emphasis on the use of performance information for budgeting in the United States is a phenomenon that has surfaced both in the federal government and in state and local governments during the 1990s. Three countries—Great Britain, Australia, and New Zealand—are among those generally considered to be at the forefront of performance-based management reform (Organization for Economic Cooperation and Development, 1995). These countries have, to varying degrees, embraced what has been generically termed the "new public management," characterized by the following principles:

Making government leaner and smaller (each of these nations, dealing with large budget deficits or government budgets determined, in varying degrees, to be out of control)

Rethinking what government does and how it does it, including introducing competitive pressures within government (either through turning over government activities to the private sector or through making increasing use of contractual arrangements for the delivery of public services)

Replacing detailed input controls (often accompanying the use of line-item budgets) with systems that provide greater flexibility to use resources for the achievement of desired results

Adopting a greater performance orientation, which includes using performance information to allocate resources, to manage those resources, and to report to citizens and other stakeholders on the results of government programs

Soliciting greater participation and input from citizens concerning their expectations of government, as well as their ex post evaluations of government performance

Although a full recitation of the specifics of these reforms cannot be attempted here, comparing some characteristics of the Australian and New Zealand cases offers some insights into the applicability of these reforms in the context of the United States. Campos and Pradhan (1996), who have studied the reforms in Australia and New Zealand in some detail, made the following points that seem particularly relevant. First, there was a very specific desire to shrink the size of government in each of these cases. This was particularly true in New Zealand, which was "a heavily interventionist state not dissimilar from former Eastern European centrally-planned economies" (Campos and Pradhan, 1996, p. 21).

Second, both countries sought to alter incentives by holding key players accountable for the achievement of particular fiscal outcomes. In New Zealand, the accountability principle is particularly prevalent—chief executives have contracts that specify levels of output, budgetary appropriations are based on the number of outputs purchased, and there is "full and frequent disclosure" of progress.

Third, both countries have engaged in considerable devolution to line agencies to perform their tasks. In Australia, for example, lump sum budgeting has replaced line item budgeting; managers have complete flexibility in the allocation of costs across different types of input, such as staffing. Furthermore, a practice known as portfolio budgeting gives line agencies the responsibility for setting priorities—for example, for identifying the spending and savings measures necessary to meet aggregate fiscal targets, which are set at the center.

There are many similarities between the problems identified in these three countries and those most often cited by critics of management in the United States. In particular, lack of flexibility for managers and the lack of accountability for results are two oft-cited weaknesses of the management environment in this country. Before discussing reform efforts in the United States in more detail, however, it seems important to cite at least two contextual differences between the situation present in these countries and the United States:

There is no clear consensus in the United States concerning the size of government. This may seem a surprising statement to Americans who are used to hearing that there is general consensus that government, at all levels, is too large. But this expression may simply reflect a desire for low taxes and high service levels. Furthermore, the expenditures of government in the United States do not approach the levels experienced by many other Organization for Economic Cooperation and Development (OECD) countries, particularly New Zealand. This means that the case for shedding significant activities is less compelling.

The fragmented nature of the U.S. political system makes any changes much more difficult to pursue. Great Britain, New Zealand, and Australia are all parliamentary systems. New Zealand, which has adopted the most radical reforms in public management, has a unitary, rather than a federal, system. It would not be easy to pursue such reforms in the U.S. political context, with extreme vertical (the division of responsibilities between levels of government) and horizontal (the separation of powers—legislative, executive, and judicial) fragmentation of authority.

The National Government in the United States

The difficulty of pursuing reform in the United States notwithstanding, several events are occurring concurrently in the U.S. national government that contribute to the improved environment for using performance measures in budgeting. Since 1990, Congress has focused more legislative attention on the measurement of results than perhaps at any time in our history. This interest first manifested itself through the passage of the Chief Financial Officers' (CFO) Act. The CFO Act's main focus is the improvement of federal financial management. Also, the act includes a provision that requires agency CFOs to develop "systematic measures of performance" for programs in their agencies (Riley, 1995, section 902, p. 6). It also instructs CFOs "to prepare and submit to the agency head timely reports" and requires that financial statements "shall reflect results of operations" (section 902, p. 6; section 303, p. 12).

More directly, the Government Performance and Results Act (GPRA) was passed by Congress and signed by President Clinton in 1993. The GPRA is the culmination of several years of effort, mainly focused in the Senate Committee on Governmental Affairs, to direct federal agencies to measure outcomes more systematically. The bill directs all federal agencies to engage in strategic planning, objective-setting, and performance measurement. Furthermore, beginning in fiscal year 1999, performance measures would be required to be reported in the budget for all federal programs. The bill also has an explicit connection to the budget allocation process, because it envisions a set of pilots in "performance budgeting." Performance budgets would present varying levels of performance resulting from different budgeted levels. At least five agencies would be required to participate in these pilot projects, which would run for fiscal years 1998 and

1999. The director of the Office of Management and Budget would report on the results of the performance budgeting pilots no later than March 31, 2001 (Joyce, 1993).

The cause of federal performance measurement was also given a major boost by the report of Vice President Gore's National Performance Review (NPR), which advocated a reduction of hierarchical controls over administrative processes in favor of empowering managers and holding them accountable for results (Gore, 1993a; Kamensky, 1996). As a part of this overall strategy, the NPR has supported a conversion from a budgeting system focused on inputs to a system that focuses on results. The goal of this exercise would be to make budgetary choices not on the basis of a comparison of the dollars provided for one activity versus another, but on the basis of a comparison of the value of the results that are expected to be achieved from providing funding for one activity versus another. The NPR also embraces the goals of the CFO Act and the GPRA (Gore, 1993b).

In all three of these cases, performance measures have a prominent role in reporting on accomplishments (the CFO Act) and in managing current resources and planning for the allocation of resources in the future (the GPRA and the NPR). This prominence, however, may overshadow some of the challenges inherent in developing measures of performance. The task of developing measures pales in comparison to the challenge inherent in trying to use performance measures as a basis for budget decision making. It is only through confronting these challenges that performance measures can eventually pay the dividends that their advocates—both within and outside government—have promised.

State and Local Governments in the United States

There is no uniform effort in state and local governments in the United States that mirrors the national effort toward more performance measurement. The general consensus, however, is that many state and local governments arrived first and have made more progress in performance measurement than the federal government. Some well-publicized cases, such as Sunnyvale, California, Phoenix, Arizona, and the state of Oregon provided important spurs to the national government effort.

For example, Sunnyvale, the highest profile local government success story, has used an elaborate performance-based system since the late 1970s. The system, according to participants, seems to promote attention to results rather than inputs, and seems to be used by both agency managers and policymakers. It also engages in long-term planning, setting overall goals and objectives as many as twenty years in advance (Lewcock, 1991). The success of the system in Sunnyvale seems to be promoted by the lack of significant resource constraints, as well as a stable vision concerning long-term goals for the jurisdiction. There is some question, therefore, about the replicability of the Sunnyvale system in other venues.

Oregon, one of the two or three most often cited state success stories (others frequently mentioned include Texas and Florida) began its current effort to improve performance management in the late 1980s. The first step was the state's engagement in a long-range planning process called Oregon Benchmarks, designed to develop a set of targets—broader societal goals—for the state into the next century (Oregon Progress Board, 1997). Concurrently (but somewhat separately), Oregon engaged in an ambitious effort to increase the use of performance measures in the budget process, in part in response to a tax limitation initiative that was likely to have a significant impact on the state budget.

The Governmental Accounting Standards Board (GASB) has provided an impetus for performance measurement in state and local government through its advocacy of service efforts and accomplishments (SEA) reporting, which emphasizes the results of government activity rather than the activities themselves (Hatry and Fountain, 1990). The GASB encourages local and state governments subscribing to its standards to improve their reporting of performance, has provided prototype indicators for several service areas, and has recommended ways in which these measures can be used to evaluate performance for government programs.

Assumptions Underlying Performance-Based Budgeting in the Context of Public Administration Theory and Practice

Performance-based budgeting, as an effort to connect resources used with results achieved, is unambiguously desirable but quite complicated to carry out in practice. Successful performance-based budgeting rests on three necessary building blocks. First, enough consensus must exist concerning the objectives of public programs for managers to effectively administer and evaluate them. Second, the measures necessary to the enterprise must be obtained—both the measures of inputs (such as dollars expended for given activities) and measures of the results achieved from governmental activities that can enable program managers and external constituencies to determine the extent to which the programs are meeting these objectives. Third, these measures must be used to inform the governmentwide resource allocation system to transform budgeting from an input-centered process to a results-oriented process. Each of these three claims is worthy of systematic scrutiny. In particular, we should examine each in the context of what past and current practice can tell us about their likelihood for success.

Can Objectives Be Agreed Upon?

The ability to measure performance is inexorably related to a clear understanding of what an agency or program is trying to accomplish. The task of clarifying those goals is much more difficult for public-sector agencies than for private corporations. Public-sector agencies operate in an environment in which they are usually asked to respond to many actors, including legislative bodies, elected executives, and the general public. Not all of these actors agree on the objectives of the agency or program.

Just as it was in Woodrow Wilson's time, it is crucial to the reformers' argument that the ends of government—that is, the desired results—can be specified in a way that provides clear direction to program managers. The task of reinventing government, then, is one of devising processes by which the ends of government should be achieved through use of the best means. Most program managers exist in an environment that is rife with goal ambiguity. Conflicting or ambiguous signals may be sent in legislation, and important actors, such as elected officials, political executives, legislative bodies (which rarely, if ever, speak with one voice), professional and scientific organizations, and citizens may not be of much help in clarifying matters.

By making the assumption that ends can be separated from means, the "reinventing government" movement also may be reinventing an idea that is more than a century old—the idea that politics (the "what" of government) can be separated from administration (the "how" of government). The separation of politics and administration and the search for sound principles of management for government trace their roots to scholars such as Wilson and Frank Goodnow. Goodnow laid the foundation for the politics-administration dichotomy through dividing the activities of government into two types—the expression of will (politics) and the execution of will (administration) (Goodnow, 1900). But if the ends of government cannot be easily agreed upon, or if considerable discretion exists for agency managers to redefine those ends in the administrative process, the challenges to goal convergence are more substantial than has typically been acknowledged.

The orthodox view of a politics-administration dichotomy and of scientific principles has been thoroughly discredited as an explanation of, and a prescription for, contemporary governmental activity. At least two arguments first presented by scholars in the 1940s challenge the efficacy of the "reinventing government" ideals. First, the dichotomy (and reinventing government) relies on an explicit assumption that general principles can be developed for public administrative activities. Half a century ago, Robert Dahl cautioned that administration lay outside of the realm of science primarily because normative values, human behavior, and contextual circumstance cannot be excluded from administrative processes (Dahl, 1947). Second, the argument that politics can be taken out of administration runs counter to the reality of administrative discretion. It is simply a fact of twentieth-century government that many nontechnical decisions are left in the hands of unelected bureaucrats; the making of these decisions *is* policymaking (see Waldo, 1948).

The key problem is the failure to recognize the essential differences between the public and the private sectors. Consider the subtitle of David Osborne and Ted Gaebler's (1992) best-selling book on reinventing government: *How the Entrepreneurial Spirit Is Transforming the Public Sector.* The assumption here is not only that a set or principles can be developed for government, but that these principles are, by and large, to be gained from the example of private business. Not all business principles, however, are directly relevant to organizing and managing for the purpose of governing (Allison, 1994).

Writing in this vein, Rosenbloom argues that public administration theory contains at least three different approaches—managerial, political, and legal—and that these approaches reflect the constitutional separation of powers—executive, legislative, and judicial (Rosenbloom, 1983). Each of the approaches emphasizes a legitimate core value—efficiency for the managerial approach, responsiveness for the political, and individual rights for the legal. Any attempt to manage the government by emphasizing only one of these values will inevitably create conflict with the other two. An emphasis on business principles, says Rosenbloom, is fully consistent with the managerial approach but runs the risk of ignoring other important values (Rosenbloom, 1983). The essential "public" nature of public programs contributes to the difficulty in agreeing on clear objectives for government programs. Laws are often drafted that are intentionally ambiguous, and contradictions often exist between laws governing programs. These ambiguities and contradictions exist because they are required to achieve the consensus necessary for laws to be adopted. But this necessary consensus-building device is inefficient. It impedes the ability of agency managers to have precise guidance concerning what elected officials want out of a program. At other times, the courts may intervene because laws or policies that may be either efficient or politically responsive nonetheless trample on the rights of individuals.

Because objectives in the public sector are open to legitimate debate and interpretation, one of the greatest obstacles to federal performance measurement involves resolving just what the objectives and priorities of an agency or program are. While this, as noted above, is a precarious process, in practice goal ambiguity does not bring government to a grinding halt. Managers fill in the details as best they can, often by trying to determine whose signals are most crucial to follow. The extent to which this leads to the kind of stability needed for effective strategic planning depends on the extent to which these agency judgments are subject to constant revision, as important actors subsequently disagree with agency judgments.

Can We Develop Measures of Budgeting Inputs and Program Results?

Connecting resources used with results achieved assumes that we can measure each. In practice, however, the measurement enterprise is fraught with difficulty, because it is troublesome to derive the true cost of government activities, organized by program, and it is at least as challenging to measure progress toward the end results of government (even if some stable consensus exists concerning what a given agency or program is supposed to accomplish).

Measuring Inputs. To know how much it costs to administer a given program, one has to be able to completely and accurately estimate the costs of that program. In large and complex organizations, this task is often quite formidable. In private sector firms, activities are organized into *cost centers* (Anthony and Young, 1994). In public sector organizations, this may imply that activities (and therefore costs) are organized into *programs*. In either case, it is necessary to capture not only the direct costs (the costs associated with individuals managing and staffing the program directly, for example), but the indirect costs as well (for example, the portion of central administrative costs—budgeting, personnel, and computing—that can be allocated to the relevant program).

The difficulty of appropriately measuring indirect costs (or, at least, the failure to do so) is an enduring obstacle to performance-based budgeting. However, without a method of measuring full costs that is consistent across government activities, the information used for budgeting will be biased. Therefore, it is at least as important to concentrate on developing appropriate measures of inputs as it is to focus on appropriate measures of results.

Measuring Results. Many agencies concentrate on measures of workload or activity because it is hard to find acceptable measures of the achievement of a policy's objectives that are also under the control of program managers. Thus, what are often dubbed performance measures are often measures of *output*, rather than measures of *outcome*. It is much easier for the Internal Revenue Service to measure assistance to taxpayers according to how many phone calls were answered than by determining the quality of the assistance given. It is much easier for the Environmental Protection Agency to measure its success according to the number of violations of agency regulations than according to air and water quality. While output measures have the virtue of being under the control of agency managers, they are of limited usefulness because they do not focus on ultimate results.

As a practical matter, public agencies are not all alike. Different solutions exist for the performance measurement problem in different agencies. Any search for performance measures should be activity-specific. Furthermore, developing measures of results is a complex business; and the ease with which they can be developed differs substantially from program to program. It is far from safe to assume that appropriate measures of results can be developed, even if objectives can be agreed upon.

Can Performance Measures Be Used for Budgeting?

Even if the obstacles to reaching agreement on objectives and to developing measures of inputs and results can be overcome, this does not solve the problem of actually *using* performance measures for budgeting. Past experience should introduce a measure of humility as we attempt to examine the likelihood that the current efforts will be successful.

The 1990s-era attempt to improve the linkage of performance measurement and budgeting is a logical successor to three similar attempts to use performance information for budgeting over the past forty years, namely performance budgeting, program budgeting (particularly as manifested through the federal government's planning-programming-budgeting system, or PPBS), and zero-based budgeting (ZBB). At least two of these (program budgeting and ZBB) attempted to budget on the basis of program results. In general, these systems fell short of their goals. In particular, the substantial effort that went into these systems failed to change the way federal resources were allocated.

The designers of each of these reforms tried to mandate a solution to federal budgeting and management by linking the budget to intended outcomes. Several important lessons emerged from their failures. First, such budgeting systems may prove antithetical to traditional incremental budgeting, and they might be resisted by those who have some stake in the process that is already in place. Budgeting, according to this argument, is about politics, and one cannot talk about reforming budget processes independently of talking about affecting the political process (Wildavsky, 1988). Allen Schick, in his classic post-mortem on PPBS, listed the following reasons among those that contributed to the failure of the system to live up to its promise (Schick, 1973):

- It was introduced across the board without much preparation.
- It was not given adequate resources, and top managers were not entirely committed to it.
- Good analysts and data were in short supply, and they were necessary to produce the kind of information crucial to the success of PPBS.
- Because PPBS was intended to require a review of all activities in each year, the reform caused so much conflict that the political system was not capable of handling it.
- PPBS was an executive budget system and largely ignored the role of the Congress in the budget process. The result was that the Congress ignored the system in favor of its established procedures.

The fact that performance-based budgeting did not gain widespread acceptance in the past is not reason enough to discount its potential. However, even if both legislative and executive branches were committed to it, and a genuine effort was undertaken to embrace a results-oriented approach to government budgeting, a fundamental dilemma remains. Simply put, it is not clear how performance measures should be used to allocate resources. For example, one cannot simply reward those agencies whose measures indicate good performance (performance in excess of some agreed-upon target, for example) and take resources away from those whose measures indicate bad performance. A thorough understanding of all of the factors (including the level of funding) that contribute to negative or positive performance is necessary before we can begin to understand how performance measures can be used to allocate resources. Performance measures, in other words, are not substitutes for more detailed program evaluation, although they may provide clues that will assist in a more efficient allocation of scarce evaluation resources.

Ultimately, if every program had performance measures, policymakers could understand the tradeoffs inherent in spending money on two competing programs. For example, if the choice was between a job-training and an air-pollution program, we might know that adding $100 million more to the budget of the Environmental Protection Agency would make the air cleaner by x amount while costing y amount of lost wages from workers who had not been trained. If we had all of these data (and we believed them), that would make decisions more informed. But it still would not necessarily make the choices easier.

The more that attempts are made to tie performance measures to the budget, the more important it is to use the correct measures and collect accurate information. The higher the stakes are, however, the greater the incentives are for people to identify self-serving measures and report misleading data. Without a process of ensuring that the appropriate measures are chosen and reported accurately, performance measurement will never deliver on its promise. When performance measures become only a more sophisticated means of agency budget justification, they cease to be useful policymaking tools. The obvious implication is that verifying the accuracy of reported data is an essential part of the measurement process.

The Current State of Performance-Based Budgeting

What are the current prospects for overcoming the obstacles to using performance measures for budgeting? Are objectives more readily agreed to? Have accounting systems been improved enough? Is performance information adequate? Are decision makers prepared to use more information on results when making budget decisions? In each case, progress has been made, but the struggle is still slow and uphill. In general, the national government faces more serious obstacles than state and local governments.

The Federal Government. Considerable disagreement continues concerning program objectives. If anything, the problems have been highlighted even more by the tension that has characterized the failure to come to grips with a plan to achieve a balanced budget for the federal government. The underlying disagreements between Congress and the President that sank such a plan in 1995 were about nothing less than a different vision about both what government should do and what level of government should do it. (See Hager and Pianin, 1997, for a good discussion of the difficulty of making substantial long-term reductions in the federal deficit.) In such an environment, it would not be surprising if program managers were even more in want of clear signals. Moreover, since many programs were under fundamental attack, managers did not have the luxury of assuming that the status quo was a desired outcome for many policymakers.

Second, it continues to be true that, without some way to better account for costs, it is very hard to relate expenditures to performance, because it is difficult to know with any certainty what costs are. Federal accounting systems—if they can be so termed in an environment where there are multiple accounting systems within many single agencies (Office of Management and Budget, 1996)—still fall substantially short of permitting full cost accounting. The federal government's accounting systems are also well behind those employed by state and local governments, which increasingly comply with generally accepted accounting principles.

There is, however, some indication of progress in federal accounting. Groups such as the Federal Accounting Standards Advisory Board (FASAB) and the Joint Financial Management Improvement Project have been toiling continuously in an effort to bring better financial management to the federal government. The FASAB is in the process of issuing standards that will require federal agencies to engage in cost accounting (Bramlett, 1991). In addition, the execution of the Chief Financial Officers' Act of 1990 fostered considerable modernization of federal financial systems and is in part focused on the creation of financial data that can be integrated with performance data, as performance-based budgeting would require. Many agencies are experimenting with reforms such as activity-based costing, which specifically focuses on connecting the discrete work products of agencies with what it costs to produce those work products. Although activity-based costing is a second-best substitute for full cost accounting, it has the virtue of being easier to implement and is thus much more likely to be useful to a greater number of agencies within a shorter period of time.

The Office of Management and Budget, in particular, is at the center of the federal government's effort to coordinate its multifront effort geared toward improved financial management. From the perspective of performance-based budgeting, perhaps the most significant development has been the issuance of a FASAB-developed standard for cost accounting in July 1995 (Office of Management and Budget, 1996). A crucial component of the implementation of this cost accounting standard is the integration of cost accounting with the requirements of GPRA, including recognizing the full costs of achieving outputs and outcomes. A prerequisite for the linking of cost accounting to program results is the development of an improved, program-based account structure for the federal government; the current account structure has no logical and consistent basis and is simply not conducive to program-based cost accounting and decision making (General Accounting Office, 1995b).

Third, many federal agencies continue to struggle to develop measures of results. There is no shortage of activity and interest. GPRA spawned more than seventy pilot projects in performance measurement. Early reviews of those pilot projects suggested several problems with the measures in many agencies. The measures used were often not tied to legislative purpose or agency mission and were often limited in scope, emphasizing workload or activity data over measures of results. Agencies avoided using measures over which agencies felt that they had limited control (National Academy of Public Administration, 1994). The bottom line is that the biggest challenge in the 1990s is a familiar one—the replacement of workload measures with measures of results.

Fourth, there has been no widespread increase in the use of performance information for resource allocation. The implication of a system with less control over inputs and more over outcomes is that the legislative branch—and budget controllers (read OMB) in the executive branch as well—should also be less control oriented and should permit agencies greater flexibility. Certainly, running through the recommendations of the National Performance Review is the notion that the Office of Management and Budget and Congress engage in excessive micromanagement of agencies. As an NPR report notes, "Excessively detailed limitations are restrictions on spending money that are not needed for policy control, take away the manager's capacity to perform, and impede the accomplishment of results" (Gore, 1993b, p. 27). In response to this, the NPR recommended numerous changes that would involve fewer congressional earmarks, less itemization of appropriation bills, and more agency autonomy in decision making.

Newcomer (1995) examined the performance information included in the fiscal year 1996 budget for four agencies—the departments of Commerce, Interior, Justice, and Treasury—and found evidence that these agencies were reporting performance data. While the majority of these data were workload data, there was a dramatic increase in the number of measures from those that had been reported in the FY95 budget. As Newcomer points out, there is, however, a big difference between having performance data (even if these data were outcome-based, which they are not in many cases) and using these data for budget decisions.

On this latter score, there is evidence that the Office of Management and Budget (OMB) has emphasized performance information much more extensively in the process of reviewing agency budgets. An OMB reorganization (called "OMB 2000"), combining many of the management and budget functions, was designed in large part to introduce more information on agency management and accomplishment into budget deliberations (General Accounting Office, 1995a). OMB guidance to agencies on preparation of budgets has increasingly emphasized performance data. Performance reviews between OMB and the agencies were held in both 1995 and 1996, and these reviews, according to participants, clearly focused on evaluating the accomplishments of programs relative to their missions. Furthermore, in the context of the 1998 budget, OMB will be conducting a "dry run" of the performance reporting that GPRA requires be included as part of the budget a year later.

The congressional response to the reinventing government movement has been mixed. Although the passage of GPRA is itself cited as evidence that Congress is interested in performance measurement, there was little knowledge of it outside of the Senate Governmental Affairs and House Government Operations Committees, at least prior to 1997. In the early 1990s, the Congress had been eager to embrace the broad goals of reinvention (a government that works better and costs less) but had not been as eager to embrace the details (Foreman, 1995). As the deadline for the filing of the GPRA performance plans nears, however, there is some indication of a greater interest in Congress, which may see GPRA as a tool that can be used to hold executive agencies more accountable (the Congressional Institute even features GPRA prominently on its World Wide Web site on the Internet).

State and Local Experience. Much of the impetus for performance-based budgeting comes from those who believe that it has been successfully applied in local and state governments. Actual experience has been somewhat spotty. In total, there have probably been greater advances in the development of performance measures for state and local governments than in the national government, but there is still scant evidence of the use of performance information for resource allocation.

Evidence on state and local performance-based budgeting comes from a number of sources. First, reports were issued in 1993 by both the General Accounting Office (GAO) and the Congressional Budget Office (CBO). The GAO study focused on five states—Connecticut, Hawaii, Iowa, Louisiana, and North Carolina—chosen because surveys and other reports had listed them as among national leaders in developing performance measures (General Accounting Office, 1993). The CBO study reported results based on site visits to four local governments (Dayton, Ohio; Charlotte, North Carolina; St. Petersburg, Florida; and Portland, Oregon) and two state governments (Florida and Oregon) that are currently using performance measurement (Congressional Budget Office, 1993). Although all of the units of government studied by GAO and CBO used some form of performance measures, most were focused on the activities of agencies rather than on results. As for connections to the budget process, the following statement by GAO researchers is probably a good statement of the "bottom line" of both reports:

> Despite long-standing efforts in states regarded as leaders in performance budgeting, performance measures have not attained sufficient credibility to influence resource allocation decisions. Instead, according to most of the state legislative and executive branch officials we interviewed, resource allocation decisions continue to be driven, for the most part, by traditional budgeting practices. . . . Outside the budget process, state officials say that performance measures have aided managers in (1) establishing program priorities, (2) strengthening management improvement efforts, (3) dealing with the results of budgetary reductions, and (4) gaining more flexibility in allocating appropriated funds (General Accounting Office, 1993, p. 1).

More recently, Broom and McGuire (1995) evaluated performance measurement efforts in five states—Texas, Oregon, Minnesota, Virginia, and Florida. This review is largely consistent with the GAO and CBO results listed earlier. That is, it identified impressive efforts to develop better performance information, in some cases (particularly Oregon) linked to the achievement of broader societal goals. It also found some cases where performance measures were specifically linked to a reform of the budget process (especially in Texas, but also in Virginia), but little evidence that performance information is actually used in the process of making budget decisions, at least at a governmentwide level.

In general, the conclusions suggested little evidence of the much-touted advances in performance-based budgeting in local and state governments. At all levels of government, however, performance measures seemed to be used in individual agencies to influence the use of resources and are a valuable management tool.

It is probably in the area of reporting that the most consistent general trend toward the development of state and local performance measures can be found. Here, the GASB Service Efforts and Accomplishments (SEA) initiative encourages state and local governments to include statements of service results in their annual financial reports. This is a significant step for an organization such as GASB, which has historically devoted itself to issues of accounting and financial reporting. It foreshadows a time when financial reports will include not only statements of how resources were expended but what was gained from the expenditure of these funds. The clear assumption is that the requirement that SEA information be reported will carry with it a greater attention to performance in policymaking. The SEA initiative has already generated substantial activity among states and local governments, but it has also been criticized in some circles (Harris, 1995) as unworkable or even foolhardy. The SEA effort, however, remains an important part of the environment for linkages of performance information and the budget at the state and local level.

Conclusion

So far, most evidence points to limitations in using performance information for governmentwide resource allocation. The limited potential of performance measures to influence budget outcomes directly does not, however, mean that they have no place in the budget process. Performance measures can be used to assist agencies in the management of a relatively fixed level of resources. For example, an agency's total funding level may be fairly stable, but it may use a performance measurement system to allocate funds among geographic or functional subunits. Performance measures can also be used to present information on the relationship between inputs and outcomes. This would define for policymakers the relationship between given levels of inputs and the results expected from them. It should be emphasized, however, that it is one thing to present such information to decision makers, but it is quite another for them to use it.

If performance measures are to be used to influence the allocation of resources, the change is not likely to happen suddenly. Rather, it may be the result of a change in culture that starts with the development of better, valid performance information at the agency level and with the reporting of that information for nonbudgetary purposes. Once this information is in the public domain, it is entirely possible that it will be more accepted and eventually used by decision makers for informing the allocation of resources.

In this context, it is not at all alarming that greater strides have not been made in performance-based budgeting. Indeed, it should be expected that the process of using performance information to allocate resources, if it is to occur at all, would take some time. Observers should not be too quick to dismiss this effort at performance-based budgeting as merely a repeat of the past failures, such as program budgeting. Key strengths of the current effort are its deliberate nature and its recognition that the *use* of performance information must wait for the development of the measures themselves.

With that said, there are challenges to performance-based government that are particularly acute in the U.S. political context, where governments at the national and state levels are almost universally organized around the constitutional principle of the separation of powers. The task of determining objectives and devising policies to further the achievement of those objectives is much simpler in a context where the political environment invites clarity of purpose for managers. This clarity of purpose is present in many parliamentary systems (such as Australia and New Zealand); it is also present in many council-manager local governments in the United States. Perhaps it is not surprising that these are the governmental units where performance-based budgeting has experienced its greatest reported success. But the U.S. constitutional and political traditions, particularly at the national and state levels, work against this kind of clarity, because objectives are open to constant interpretation and reinterpretation at every stage of the policy process.

Performance-based budgeting still must exist in an arena that is political, that is dominated by strong personalities, and that has uncertainty as the only constant. Even if it is not true, to paraphrase Wildavsky's statement that "no one knows how to do" performance-based budgeting (see Wildavsky, 1969, p. 193), it is at least true that there are substantial obstacles to developing the accounting systems, the performance measures, and the incentives for decision making that would be necessary to implement it.

References

Allison, G. "Public and Private Management: Are They Fundamentally Alike in All Unimportant Respects?" In F. Lane (ed.), *Current Issues in Public Administration.* (5th ed.) New York: St. Martin's Press, 1994.

Anthony, R., and Young, D. *Management Control in Nonprofit Organizations.* (5th ed.) Homewood, Ill.: Irwin, 1994.

Bramlett, R. W. "The Federal Accounting Standards Advisory Board: An Introduction for Non-Accountants." *Public Budgeting and Finance,* 1991, *11* (4), 11–19.

Broom, C., and McGuire, L. "Performance-Based Government Models: Building a Track Record." *Public Budgeting and Finance,* 1995, *15* (4), 3–17.

Campos, E., and Pradhan, S. "Budgetary Institutions and Expenditure Outcomes." Policy Research Working Paper #1646. Washington, D.C.: World Bank Policy Research Department, Sept. 1996.

Congressional Budget Office. *Using Performance Measures in the Federal Budget Process.* Washington, D.C.: U.S. Government Printing Office, 1993.

Dahl, R. "The Science of Administration: Three Problems." *Public Administration Review,* 1947, 7 (1), 1–11.

Foreman, C. "The NPR Meets Congress." In D. Kettl and J. DiIulio, Jr. (eds.), *Inside the Reinvention Machine: Appraising Governmental Reform.* Washington, D.C.: The Brookings Institution, 1995.

General Accounting Office. *Performance Budgeting: State Experiences and Implications for the Federal Government.* Washington, D.C.: General Accounting Office, 1993.

General Accounting Office. *Office of Management and Budget: Changes Resulting from the OMB 2000 Reorganization.* Washington, D.C.: General Accounting Office, 1995a.

General Accounting Office. *Budget Account Structure: A Descriptive Overview.* Washington, D.C.: General Accounting Office, 1995b.

Goodnow, F. *Politics and Administration.* New York: Russell and Russell, 1900.

Gore, A., Jr. *Creating a Government That Works Better and Costs Less.* Washington, D.C.: U.S. Government Printing Office, 1993a.

Gore, A., Jr. *Mission Driven, Results Oriented Budgeting.* Washington, D.C.: U.S. Government Printing Office, 1993b.

Hager, G., and Pianin, E. *Mirage.* Washington, D.C.: Congressional Quarterly Press, 1997.

Harris, J. "Service Efforts and Accomplishments Standards: Fundamental Questions of an Emerging Concept." *Public Budgeting and Finance,* 1995, *15* (4), 18–37.

Hatry, H., and Fountain, J. *Service Efforts and Accomplishments Reporting: Its Time Has Come, An Overview.* Norwalk, Conn.: Governmental Accounting Standards Board, 1990.

Joyce, P. G. "Using Performance Measures in the Federal Budget Process: Proposals and Prospects." *Public Budgeting and Finance,* 1993, *13* (4), 3–17.

Kamensky, J. "Role of the 'Reinventing Government' Movement in Federal Management Reform." *Public Administration Review,* 1996, *56* (3), 247–255.

Lewcock, T. F. Statement before the Senate Committee on Governmental Affairs, 102nd Congress, May 12, 1991.

National Academy of Public Administration. *Toward Useful Performance Measurement: Lessons Learned from Initial Pilot Performance Plans Under the Government Performance and Results Act.* Washington, D.C.: National Academy of Public Administration, 1994.

Newcomer, K. E. "Performance Measurement in the Federal Budgetary Process: Will It Stick This Time?" Paper presented at the 56th annual conference of the American Society for Public Administration, San Antonio, Tex., July 1995.

Office of Management and Budget. *Federal Financial Management Status Report and Five-Year Plan.* Washington, D.C.: U.S. Government Printing Office, 1996.

Oregon Progress Board. *Oregon Shines II: Updating Oregon's Strategic Plan.* Salem: Oregon Progress Board, 1997.

Organization for Economic Cooperation and Development. *Governance in Transition: Public Management Reforms in OECD Countries.* Paris: Organization for Economic Cooperation and Development, 1995.

Osborne, D., and Gaebler, T. *Reinventing Government.* Reading, Mass.: Addison-Wesley, 1992.

Riley, A. C. "Reporting of Performance Measures for Federal Agencies: The Initial Impact of the Chief Financial Officer (sic) Act of 1990." *International Journal of Public Administration,* 1995, *18* (2 and 3), 521–580.

Rosenbloom, D. "Public Administrative Theory and the Separation of Powers." *Public Administration Review,* 1983, *43* (3), 219–227.

Schick, A. "A Death in the Bureaucracy: The Demise of Federal PPB." *Public Administration Review,* 1973, *33* (2), 146–156.

Waldo, D. *The Administrative State.* New York: The Ronald Press Company, 1948.

Wildavsky, A. "Rescuing Policy Analysis From PPBS." *Public Administration Review,* 1969, *29* (2), 189–202.

Wildavsky, A. *The New Politics of the Budgetary Process.* Glenview, Ill.: Scott, Foresman, 1988.

Philip G. Joyce is assistant professor in the Maxwell School of Citizenship and Public Affairs at Syracuse University.

Information technology is often a key factor in delivering public services well and at the lowest possible cost. This chapter presents five best practices in information technology performance management and measurement. These practices could be usefully applied in other support functions, such as financial management or human resources management.

Performance Results: The Information Technology Factor

Sharon L. Caudle

For government managers, accountability for results means that managers must achieve and sustain a high level of performance defined by customers, taxpayers, elected officials, and other organizations with which they work. Increasingly, program authorizations, operational planning, budget decisions, and resource allocations hinge on how well agencies meet performance expectations. Government managers, in response, set performance targets, design clear performance measures, measure outputs and outcomes, and use the results for policy and programmatic decision making.

Information technology (IT) products, services, and delivery processes are important resources for results-driven government agency programs. Agency managers—the managers responsible for agencywide results and operational customers in charge of a program or a support function—greatly rely on IT products and services in their mission delivery processes. These agencywide and operational customers want to know how IT products and services truly support program and function quality, costs, timeliness, and amount of work accomplished. For federal managers, legislative requirements in the Chief Financial Officers Act of 1990, the Government Performance and Results Act of 1993, the Federal Acquisition Streamlining Act of 1994, the Paperwork Reduction Act of 1995, and the Clinger-Cohen Act of 1996 (including the Information Technology Management Reform Act) expect rigorous IT performance management.

The author was the project director and primary researcher for the U.S. General Accounting Office (GAO) research described in this chapter. The findings presented in this chapter reflect the views of the author and are not intended to present the official views of the GAO.

The Paperwork Reduction Act of 1995, the overarching statute dealing with the acquisition and management of information resources (including technology), stresses that agencies should only acquire and apply information resources to support agency missions, including the delivery of services to the public. The Clinger-Cohen Act repeats this emphasis and elaborates on how agencies should acquire information technology. Under the Clinger-Cohen Act, managers must establish efficiency and effectiveness program improvement goals using IT. Performance measurements must assess how well IT supports agency programs. Agency heads must benchmark agency process performance against comparable processes in terms of cost, speed, productivity, and quality of outputs and outcomes. Agency heads must analyze agency missions and make appropriate changes in mission and administrative processes before making significant IT investments to support missions. Annual performance reports cover how well each agency improves agency operations through IT.

The Clinger-Cohen Act, plus other legislative requirements, certainly increase the pressure for federal agency managers to craft a strong IT performance management system. Crafting such a system requires federal managers to define their agency and line manager programmatic performance expectations, develop IT objectives to match those expectations, and design IT measures for the objectives. For the best performance management system, IT managers and agencywide and operational customers—program line managers and other support function managers—work together to use these IT measures to leverage and improve IT performance in ways that will improve program and support mission delivery. Traditional IT measures such as workload, machine availability, reports generated, and lines of software code generated no longer are sufficient by themselves to answer IT performance questions. What must be measured is the mission value of IT products and services.

Defining IT Performance Management—Best Practices

IT performance management is relatively new. Major research began in the late 1980s, typified by the work of Bjorn-Andersen and Davis (1986) and Strassmann and others (1988). Most of this early work attempted to define IT areas subject to measurement and specific measures themselves on a fairly broad scale. Later efforts, such as that of Carlson and McNurlin (1989), presented alternative measurement frameworks or, like Saunders and Jones (1992), reported additional research findings. However, most of these early IT measurement efforts stressed traditional IT measures such as the size of IT staff and the IT budget as a percentage of operating expenses, not the way IT contributes to mission performance. More recent work, such as that of the Society of Information Management Advanced Practices Council (1995), shows targeting of additional IT measures to include mission performance. The Office of the State Auditor (1991) in Texas, the Florida Legislature Joint Committee on Information Technology Resources (1994), the Association for Federal Information Resources Management (1995), the Government Centre for Information

Systems (1995) in the United Kingdom, the U.S. General Services Administration (1996), and the National Academy of Public Administration (1996) have issued IT performance management guidance targeted specifically at government managers.

To add to this body of work and as part of ongoing best practices research, the U.S. General Accounting Office (GAO) did field research to see how leading organizations in the private and public sectors approached IT performance management. These leading organizations included the Xerox Corporation, Eastman Kodak Company, Texas Instruments, Motorola Semiconductor Products Sector, and American Express Travel Related Services Company; the Oregon Department of Transportation; and the cities of Sunnyvale and Phoenix. The GAO research also selectively included the U.S. Immigration and Naturalization Service, the U.S. General Services Administration Information Technology Service, and the U.S. Department of Agriculture to assess early federal practices. The research also used other general and IT performance management literature and reports from many other organizations to supplement its in-depth organizational research.

The research found five key practices in building and sustaining a successful IT performance management system. They are:

Follow an IT "results chain." Leading organizations build and enforce a disciplined flow from agency goals to objectives to measures to individual accountability. (A *goal* is a broad statement regarding a desired outcome, and an *objective* is a measurable specification about the result to be accomplished within a specific time frame.) The leading organizations define specific goals, objectives, and diverse measures and develop a picture of how IT outputs and outcomes directly impact agencywide and operational customer performance needs.

Follow a balanced scorecard approach. Leading organizations use an IT goal, objective, and measure approach that covers and balances strategic and operational aspects. Four goal areas cover meeting the strategic needs of the agency; meeting the needs of individual operational customers, such as those of a specific program; addressing internal IT business performance, such as applications development and maintenance; and addressing ongoing IT innovation and learning, such as through skill development.

Target IT measures, results, and accountability at different levels of decision making. These levels cover agency executives, senior to midlevel managers responsible for program or support units, and lower-level management running specific operations or projects.

Build a comprehensive IT measure, data collection, and analysis capability. The leading organizations give considerable attention to baselining, benchmarking, and the collection and analysis of IT performance information using a variety of tools and methods. These tools and methods keep the organizations on top of IT performance and reduce the burden of data collection and analysis.

Improve IT processes meeting mission goals. In the leading organizations, IT performance improvement begins and ends with IT business processes—how the IT organization's work gets done. The organizations map their IT business processes and improve those processes most important in meeting agency and operational customer needs.

The following sections describe these practices in more detail, listing specific characteristics. A final section discusses key steps in implementing an IT performance management system.

As the reader examines and applies these five best practices, it is important to remember that an IT performance management system has to fit the organization. There is not one single best IT performance management system nor should there be. How an organization designs, implements, and sustains an IT performance management system that suits it depends on many factors. These include whether an organization's leadership, decision-making, appraisal, and reward systems support IT performance management; how important and widespread IT's use is in mission delivery; how IT activities are organized at a central and decentralized level; and the availability of performance management skills and tools. For all organizations, top management ownership of, involvement in, and use of IT performance information is vital for a successful performance management system. Also important is the partnership forged between IT managers and staff and operational customer managers to meet mission goals and objectives without working at cross-purposes.

Practice 1: Follow an Information Technology Results Chain

In leading organizations, IT products and services align with and directly support agencywide and operational goals and objectives. The leading organizations use a systematic approach through a *results chain* in linking organizational goals and objectives to the vital few IT performance measures needed to manage for effective results. The IT results chain starts with organizational goals and objectives. From these, IT management, working with agencywide and operational customers, develops an IT purpose statement and specific IT goals. Then IT management develops a vital few IT objectives for each goal and IT measures for each objective. The chain concludes with a definition of individual or team management and staff performance expectations. As the organization develops and finalizes IT goals, objectives, and measures, there is constant discussion of their purpose and benefits, data collection, and analysis and the use of measurement data to continually improve IT performance.

Define Specific Organizational Goals, Objectives, and Measures. Use of a results chain presumes an understanding of the organization's direction and expectations. Thus, measuring IT's contribution starts with a precise understanding of agencywide and operational customers' strategic plans and basic outcome performance measures. For example, the Immigration and

Naturalization Service (INS) started its IT performance management with the commissioner's annual planning priorities. In 1995, these were to strengthen border protection, to expedite removal of criminal aliens, to reduce incentives for unlawful migration, to implement asylum reform regulations, to promote and streamline naturalization, and to broaden and integrate the INS systems infrastructure. These goals were converted to program priority plans, which IT managers could then use for their own performance management effort.

Directly Map IT Goals, Objectives, and Measures to Agency Strategic Goals. In leading organizations, IT goals, objectives, and measures come directly from organizational goals and objectives. For example, Phoenix's Information Technology Department's strategic goals come from city strategies. Units within the Information Technology Department must match their goals, objectives, and measures to customer-defined goals of time, cost, and customer satisfaction. Xerox's Global Process and Information Management organization developed four strategies to meet what it called the Xerox 2000 business strategy, aiming to help reengineer Xerox business processes and develop an IT environment that would meet business requirements. INS identified an IT portfolio that will support and enhance each of its strategic goal areas, such as the way IT will support strengthening border protection.

Prepare a Description of Events and Measures to Understand IT's Contribution. Agency and operational customers focus on outcome measures—what the program has actually accomplished in comparison to its goals. IT managers often have difficulty showing how their products and services directly produce those outcomes. A helpful technique is using a description of which program events lead to other events and finally to mission outcomes, with corresponding program measures. The description shows how program inputs achieve desired results, generally progressing from intermediate outcomes to final outcomes. In support, the IT organization describes how IT products and services such as networks and software applications help the program description of events, often at the intermediate outcome level—for example, having responsive IT help desk services support a program's use of computerized applications, which in turn supports program delivery activities.

Building descriptions of events and measures with agency and operational customers can help IT managers understand exactly how IT products and services support customers, and how they should be measured—for example, the INS wanted to free up border patrol agents from paperwork to spend more time on front-line enforcement programs. It also wanted to have detailed records of illegal alien apprehensions and criminals. It used IT measures of a specific application—the number of locations and the number of records entered into an automated identification program—to support these border control goals.

Use a Variety of Measures to Evaluate IT Performance. The leading organizations use a variety of measures for IT—input, output, outcome, and a combination of measures. Input and output measures assess workload and demand for products and services. An IT input example would be the number of IT managers and staff. An output measure could be the number of IT projects completed. Outcome measures assess results compared to expectations. An IT outcome measure could be the level of customer satisfaction with IT services. Combination measures assess efficiency and effectiveness, such as the ratio of computer application availability compared to a standard, such as 99 percent availability.

In addition, leading organizations track explanatory information to use with these measures. This information describes environmental conditions that can influence IT measures. For example, a change from a mainframe environment to a client-server environment, IT policy changes, or the decentralization of IT services will cause changes in IT performance or require actual changes in measures as other measures become obsolete.

Practice 2: Follow a Balanced Scorecard Approach

A second best practice is to use a balanced scorecard approach to IT performance management. The balanced scorecard measures performance in several goal areas and forces managers to consider goal achievement within the context of the whole organization. Kaplan and Norton (1992, 1993, 1996) describe the balanced scorecard approach as one that evaluates performance in four areas: financial (how the organization looks to shareholders), customer (how customers see performance), internal business (what the organization must excel at), and innovation and learning (ability of the organization to continue to improve and create value).

Gold (1992) adapted the balanced scorecard approach for an information systems measurement framework. Many leading organizations the research studied used the scorecard approach or similar concepts. Other approaches can be found in, for example, Rubin (1994), Parker, Benson, and Trainor (1988), Strassmann (1990), and the Society for Information Management Advanced Practices Council (1995).

The research indicated that a comprehensive balanced scorecard for IT should address four key goal areas:

- Meeting the strategic needs of the agency as a whole, in contrast to specific individual operational customers within the agency
- Meeting the needs of individual operational customers with IT products and services
- Addressing internal IT business performance that delivers IT products and services for individual customers and the agency
- Addressing ongoing IT innovation and learning as IT grows and develops its skills and IT applications

The first two goal areas address whether IT is providing the right products and services for the agency and individual operational customers. The last two goal areas address how well IT is performing to deliver those products and services. Each leading organization customized a set of IT measures appropriate for its objectives within each goal area. Although the organizations did not severely limit the number of measures developed at the beginning, over time they became more focused. The use of the balanced scorecard gets rid of "safety net" measures, which organizations often collect just in case someone asks.

Goal Area 1: Meeting the Strategic Needs of the Agency. Too often in the past, IT managers and staff satisfied individual operational customers to the detriment of agency IT needs and expectations. The research indicated four strategic agency IT objective areas for this goal area. One is supporting agency mission goals. Sample measures for this first objective area are the percentage of IT strategies fully matched to agency strategies and the percentage of mission improvements attributable to IT solutions and services. A second objective area is IT portfolio analysis and management. An IT portfolio is a comprehensive inventory of computer applications that were developed or purchased to manage an organization's processes and information. Sample measures include the percentage of old applications retired and the percentage of the IT portfolio reviewed and disposed.

A third objective area is financial and investment performance, covering the management of IT costs and returns. Sample measures include the IT budget as a percentage of the agency's operational budget and compared to industry averages. The final objective area is IT resource usage, which targets how the agency can leverage and share its IT resources across the agency. Sample measures include the percentage of databases that can be shared and the percentage of hardware and software with interoperability capabilities.

Goal Area 2: Meeting the Needs of Individual Customers. The second goal area involves meeting the needs of individual operational customers, such as at the program level. The research indicated three objective areas. The first objective area under this goal is customer partnership and involvement. This objective area covers the mutual partnership aspects of the IT organization and customers in developing the best possible IT products and services. Sample measures include the percentage of cooperative customer and IT applications design and the percentage of customers attending IT investment meetings. A second objective area is customer satisfaction, which assesses how pleased customers are with IT activities. Sample measures are the percentage of customers satisfied with IT problem resolution and the percentage of error or defect levels. The last objective area is business process support, which involves recognizing the importance of business process improvement as organizations streamline and reengineer. Sample measures are the degree to which IT solutions support process improvement plans and the percentage of new users able to use applications unaided after initial training.

Goal Area 3: Addressing IT Internal Business Performance. The third goal area in the balanced scorecard recognizes that how well IT does its job on a day-to-day basis using its own business processes is what translates in large part to agency and operational customer satisfaction. IT managers and staff, along with agency senior management, decide which of the many IT business processes must excel in meeting customer needs. This goal area is where many of the traditional and still-existing IT measures fail, often focusing on the efficiency of computing and communications hardware.

The research identified four objective areas under this third goal area. The first objective area is applications development and maintenance, which measures how well IT builds agency applications and keeps them up and running. Sample measures include the percentage of reduction in development cycle times and mean time to resolve critical application defects. The second area is project performance, which examines how well IT delivers specific IT projects. Sample measures include the percentage of projects on time and on budget and compliance with cost targets.

The third objective area is IT infrastructure (that is, computer network) availability in a variety of areas. This area keeps managers on top of availability and responsiveness of IT applications that support program or other agency activities. Sample measures include the percentage of time computer services are available and on-line response time. The last objective area is agency architecture standards. An architecture defines common standards and rules for both data and technology and maps key processes and information flows. Sample measures are the number of variations from the standards and the percentage increase in systems using a standard architecture.

Goal Area 4: Addressing Innovation and Learning. The final goal area in the balanced scorecard approach promotes IT innovation and learning. It recognizes the importance of continually improving IT support to the agency and operational customers. The goal area speaks to capabilities, such as bringing new technologies to bear on customer problems, practicing the best methodologies, and retaining and developing the best employees.

The research found four objective areas for this goal. The first objective area is workforce competency and development, which involves ensuring a capable and skilled IT workforce. Sample measures include the number of staff by a specific skill area and the percentage of IT budget devoted to training and staff development. The second objective area is advanced technology use, which stresses the installation of proven, high-powered hardware and software where appropriate. Sample measures include the percentage of employees skilled in advanced technology applications and the organizational penetration of advanced technologies.

The third objective area is currency of the methodologies in the organization, such as applications development methodologies. Sample measures include the percentage of employees skilled in advanced methodologies and the dollars available to support advanced methodology use. The last objective area in the goal area is employee satisfaction and retention. It measures how well IT employees are satisfied with the quality of their work environment and general IT strategies and accomplishments. Sample measures are the percentage of employees satisfied with the technical and operating environment and the percentage of employee turnover by function.

Practice 3: Target Measures, Results, and Accountability at Decision-Making Levels

Leading organizations recognize that measures and performance reports are not "one size fits all." They tailor measurement and performance reporting for specific decision-making levels. These levels cover the agencywide or executive management level, senior to middle management level, and specific operations or a project level covered by first-line supervisors. The organizations know that decision making at these various levels calls in most cases for different measures and reports. The organizations develop an IT performance management system that can link the right measures to the right decision makers and that directly aligns with agency and operational customer goals.

Decision-Making Level IT Measures and Reports. Performance measures and reports at each management level have specific ends in mind. At the agencywide level, executives look for IT performance and measures on an annual or quarterly basis that summarize mission results, or how well IT is meeting its purpose. For example, top Xerox managers receive a quarterly report profiling IT spending. The summary can also serve as the basis for external reporting to stakeholders and the general public.

Moving to the second level of program and support units, IT measurement use switches from outcomes to more emphasis on input and output information. Input and output information tells decision makers how specific units are performing. At this level, more detailed performance information is used for the management and improvement of operations and integrating activities across IT business processes or projects. For example, Xerox division managers receive a report of the percentage of IT projects on time for their division.

At the bottom or first-line supervisor decision-making level, the measurement emphasizes projects and individual systems performance. Highly detailed tactical and execution information using input and output measures guide funding, contract development and monitoring, project priorities, and possible adjustments in program operating procedures. For example, Xerox gathers project information, such as the number of defects per thousand function points and how much it costs to provide individual workstation set-ups for employees. (A function point measures an IT application in terms of the amount of functionality it provides users. Function points count the information components of an application, such as external inputs and outputs and external interfaces.)

American Express' Technologies group has similar levels of measures. The first level is executive information that represents Technologies' overall effectiveness against company goals, such as achieving world-class time-to-market for new products, achieving world-class economics, and developing new business. IT measures include development cycle time, time requirements and cost for ongoing operations, cost of quality, and elimination of root causes of IT failures. The second level is senior and midlevel managers, where IT measures support accountability for supporting level-one goals. Measures include development cycle time and staff time. The final level is operational information for development, operations, project leaders, and other Technologies employees.

Measure Alignment and Using the Balanced Scorecard. Once an agency has the balanced scorecard goals, objectives, and potential measures mentioned in Practice 2, then it selects its final measures and places them in the specific decision-making levels mentioned previously. For example, for the innovation and learning goal area of the balanced scorecard, one objective area is workforce competency and development. A top-level measure might be the percentage of the IT budget devoted to training and staff development. A second-level measure might be the percentage of staff professionally certified in a methodology. A third-level measure might be the number of staff by skill area for a particular project.

The leading organizations also make sure that measures used at the lowest level, the specific operations or project level, directly relate to the other two levels. Only rarely will an organization have a single performance measure appropriate for all three levels. However, performance measures and information at the lowest level should directly support policy and mission strategies. Requiring different measures forestalls the temptation to "roll up" measures from lower levels on top of each other and pass the information along to higher-level officials. This approach often produces information top officials cannot digest, may hide embarrassing details in a mountain of data, and promotes the self-selection of favorable data.

Individual Accountability and IT Scorecard Goals. Tying together the IT balanced scorecard and the IT results chain mentioned means that agency managers have to ask," "Who is accountable for results, and how are they held accountable?" The leading organizations have learned that managing performance well depends on the connection between IT purpose, goals, and objectives, and the individual manager and staff actions that implement those goals. The leading organizations regularly compare IT performance against performance expectations and hold IT managers and staff and any program line managers involved accountable for IT results. IT performance details and commitments are placed in formal or informal IT performance improvement plans. These performance commitments and timelines are widely distributed to IT management and staff and operational customers. Measure and results reviews report on the actual outcomes. Individual personnel appraisals tie IT performance to merit pay, bonuses, promotional opportunities, and other incentives.

Practice 4: Build a Comprehensive Measure, Data Collection, and Analysis Capability

Building a balanced scorecard and decision-making level measures is only one step in designing an effective IT performance management system. In the leading organizations, much care and attention went to the "back end" of performance management: data collection and analysis. Although the organizations searched for existing measures and data that had already proven workable, much existing data is no longer appropriate. The leading organizations developed a clear rationale for new and continued data collection and specifications for accuracy, reliability, timeliness, and use before setting out measurement requirements. They also recognized that using multiple measures calls for a variety of data collection efforts.

Data Collection Tools. For each data collection requirement in the balanced scorecard or other frameworks, whether qualitative or quantitative, the leading organizations developed manual and automated tools to reduce the burden of collecting IT performance information. These included general observations by program and IT managers and staff, formal performance measures reports, customer satisfaction surveys and interview questions, reviews of records and documents, and automated hardware and software productivity data collection. Often, the organizations started with a primitive data collection strategy, developing data definitions and working with customers and IT staff to gain understanding and agreement. In the early stages, some of the data collection may be manual, to be supplemented or replaced later by automated systems.

Baseline and Benchmark Information. The leading organizations assessed what performance information they had for the measures they had selected (*baselining*) and how that might compare to other organizations or similar processes within their organization if there were discrete IT units (*benchmarking*). In baselining, the current performance becomes the *baseline* or standard against which further performance progress is measured. Benchmarking was done with other IT organizations in the agency, with IT organizations outside the enterprise, and with similar processes in other industries.

The leading organizations also believe consistency of hard data collection from year to year is important. Some performance information, such as computer and communications availability, customer satisfaction percentages, and software capability maturity levels, are relatively durable and comparable over longer time periods.

Performance Measure Maturity and Review. A common stumbling block for organizations is the tendency to wait for perfect measures instead of thinking in terms of improving measures over time. Each of the measures used in the balanced scorecard at the outset is generally not the best possible. Some measures are already in place and cannot be easily displaced, some data may not be available quickly or will be too burdensome to collect at present, and some objectives will require more definition.

Kodak is one organization that is systematically defining the maturity of each measure it plans to use in the balanced scorecard. Kodak categorizes measure maturity as either fundamental, growing, or maturing. *Fundamental* indicators are established ones. *Growing* measures are those evolving from the fundamental, but are not the best they can be. *Maturing* measures are defined as best-in-class for whatever is being measured. For example, for internal performance, a fundamental measure is to meet all service level agreements, a growing measure is information delivery excellence, and a maturing measure is defect-free products and services.

In addition, the leading organizations regularly assess their IT measures and data collection and analysis process to see if they are still appropriate. The reviews and audits challenge the necessity of the measures and their linkage to agency strategic plans and individual performance expectations. The reviews also analyze key performance drivers in each goal area, often questioning how changes in one area will affect results in other areas.

Concise, Understandable Performance Reporting. Lastly, the leading organizations take great care in designing IT performance reports that are concise, easy to understand, and tailored to various audiences. They judiciously use text and graphics, trend information, and explanatory information to present and explain IT performance information, often providing corrective action ideas where performance must improve.

Practice 5: Improve IT Processes Meeting Mission Goals

In the last best practice, the leading organizations make IT business process improvement a high priority because the processes deliver the IT products and services so critical to agency and operational customer performance. If IT does not have the right capability to deliver the needed products and services, organizational goals suffer.

The leading organizations improve IT processes by first identifying specific IT business processes. This helps the IT organization focus on primary activities, identify IT competencies, eliminate processes that do not add value, and facilitate IT process innovation. Some of the organizations studied developed their IT process orientation based on work done by Ernst and Young and later published by a workgroup of the Society for Information Management (SIM) (Society for Information Management Working Group on ISPA, 1993). SIM's latest version of its IT business process framework includes eight IT processes (Society for Information Management Working Group on ISPA, 1996). For example, one IT business process is to perform customer relations. This process develops and maintains working relationships with the customers of the IT products and services.

Next, the leading organizations identify which of all the IT business processes are the most important and in need of improvement. At Texas Instruments, for example, many IT customer business process reengineering activities established a clear need for rapid development of IT solutions, flexibility with respect to business rules and work flows, and cost-effective use of advanced technology. In response, the IT group developed an IT process map and focused initial improvement efforts on the process called *solutions provisioning*. Solutions provisioning assembles the hardware and software pieces together to form solutions for IT customers.

Implementation Steps

The five key practices do not happen easily or overnight. Agency managers just starting to develop IT performance management systems, or those who want to enhance existing ones, have a formidable task. They are often faced with severe resource constraints, demands for immediate IT support and solutions as program areas reduce staff and reengineer business processes, and skepticism about the value of IT performance management. The research found that three activities appear important in putting the practices in place. These are assessing organizational readiness for a successful IT performance management system and staging its development, following a simple measure selection process, and recognizing that system maturity will change over time.

Organizational Readiness. The leading organizations look for executive and senior managers' readiness to offer involvement, commitment, and day-to-day support of an IT performance management system. They also determine if they have adequate resources, including staff allocation, skills, time, tools, and use of consultants or technical assistance if needed. Organizational readiness also means existing mission and support function planning, budgeting, and evaluation processes will accept and use performance results. The agency needs the capability to specify clear agencywide and operational customer goals and objectives to set the focus and direction for IT performance. The IT organization has to understand the business of the agency and operational customers and make sure IT measures are consistent with business measures. That is, the organization must have the capability to develop a description of how IT supports those customers and build the description of program events and measures described earlier.

The organizations also determine if they have the support of other stakeholders and funding sources, such as legislative staff. If the stakeholders and funders do not have a common understanding and agreement with proposed IT goals, objectives, and measures, then the organization is not ready to develop a viable IT performance management system.

Lastly, organizational readiness means paying attention to organizational culture—is the culture receptive to data collection, measurement, and analysis and accountability for performance as part of an overall performance management system? An agency should be positive about performance management and measurement, viewing them as ways to stress quality and customer satisfaction. Often, this means an agency will have to assess existing organizational values and principles and what behavior they create toward a performance management system.

A Simple Measure Selection Process. Selecting and implementing IT performance measures is extremely complex. Each agency and its operational customers will have a mission and goals that often differ significantly from those of other agencies. A set of IT performance measures that work for one organization likely will not work as well in another agency. The performance measures differ on what is valued most in terms of IT performance. Organizations that are the most successful sift through the many possible IT goals, objectives, and measures before finalizing them in a balanced scorecard or similar framework. The sifting process assesses which goals, objectives, and measures are the most valuable to the organization currently, and which will be for at least the near future. It decides which measures are the most relevant for customer and stakeholder needs. It eliminates measures for which good quality data cannot be obtained practically.

IT Performance Management System Maturity Over Time. Lastly, the research found from the case studies and from the literature review that an IT performance management system develops maturity over time. Drawing specifically on work done for the city of Phoenix and discussed by Rubin (1991) and Doctor and Gold (1993), the research indicated three possible stages in the development of an IT performance management system.

In stage one, the IT organization wants to deliver reliable, cost-effective operations. It develops and implements a performance management system that examines internal IT operations against standards and acceptable levels of performance. It uses traditional, activity-based measures, such as number of reports issued and mainframe availability. If the IT balanced scorecard were used, the IT organization would concentrate almost totally on goal and objective areas falling in IT internal business performance.

In stage two, the IT organization wants to build competencies to consistently deliver new and improved systems. It eliminates root causes of IT defects, strives to produce IT solutions on time and within budget, and starts linking key technical measures such as computer application availability to mission performance. The goal is to improve IT processes. In this stage, the IT organization would start adding the balanced scorecard goal and objective areas of innovation and learning, supplementing internal business performance.

In stage three, the IT organization wants to aggressively apply its IT expertise in meeting agency and operational customer mission requirements. IT performance outcome requirements and accountability are put in mission delivery terms. Measures reflect customer needs and benefits, expressing measures in terms customers understand, such as program delivery results. Stage three IT organizations also specify who is responsible for corrective action. In this stage, the measures found in the strategic and operational customer goals of the balanced scorecard approach are added to the other two balanced scorecard goal and objective areas.

The maturity staging indicates that IT organizations must be good at the IT operational basics in stage one before moving successfully to stages two and three. An IT organization viewed as a failure in day-to-day operations will not have enough credibility or support within the agency to play a strategic role.

Still a Developing Area

As indicated in the beginning of this chapter, IT performance management and measurement is still relatively new. Most of the organizations contacted for this research have worked on their own IT performance management systems for several years. In many cases, new organizational directions and business or mission strategies necessitated even more rigor in the existing IT performance management system. Without exception, however, the leading organizations have a strong performance management culture for all activities, not just IT. These organizations share many similar performance management values and general mission achievement goals that mandate IT results and accountability. For these organizations, IT measures make a very positive difference in mission and business performance.

References

Association for Federal Information Resources Management. *The Connection: Linking IRM and Mission Performance.* Washington, D.C.: Association for Federal Information Resources Management, 1995.

Bjorn-Andersen, N., and Davis, G. B. (eds.). *Information Systems Assessment: Issues and Challenges.* Working Conference on Information Systems Assessment. Amsterdam: North Holland, 1986.

Carlson, W., and McNurlin, B. *Measuring the Value of Information Systems.* Rockville, Md.: I/S Analyzer, 1989.

Doctor, M. S., and Gold, C. L. *The IT Process Landscape.* Ernst & Young Total Quality Management for Information Services Leadership Program Working Paper. Boston: Ernst & Young Publishers, 1993.

Florida Legislature Joint Committee on Information Technology Resources. *Information System Performance Measurement: A Method for Enhancing Accountability in State Information Systems.* Tallahassee, Fla.: Joint Committee on Information Technology Resources, 1994.

Gold, C. L. *IS Measures—A Balancing Act.* Boston: Ernst & Young Center for Information Technology and Strategy, 1992.

Government Centre for Information Systems. *Benchmarking IS/IT.* London: HMSO, 1995.

Kaplan, R. S., and Norton, D. P. "The Balanced Scorecard—Measures That Drive Performance." *Harvard Business Review,* 1992, *70* (1), 71–79.

Kaplan, R. S., and Norton, D. P. "Putting the Balanced Scorecard to Work." *Harvard Business Review,* 1993, *70* (5), 134–147.

Kaplan, R. S., and Norton, D. P. "Using the Balanced Scorecard as a Strategic Management System." *Harvard Business Review,* 1996, *74* (1), 75–85.

National Academy of Public Administration. *Information Management Performance Measures.* Washington, D.C.: National Academy of Public Administration, 1996.

Office of the State Auditor. *A Guide to Measure the Performance of Information Systems.* Austin, Tex.: Office of the State Auditor, 1991 (SAO Report no. 1-112).

Parker, M. M., Benson, R. J., and Trainor, H. E. *Information Economics: Linking Business Performance to Information Technology.* Englewood Cliffs, N.J.: Prentice Hall, 1988.

Rubin, H. "Measure for Measure." *Computerworld,* Apr. 15, 1991, pp. 77–78.

Rubin, H. A. "In Search of the Business Value of Information Technology." *Application Development Trends,* Nov. 1994, pp. 23–27.

Saunders, C. S., and Jones, J. W. "Measuring the Performance of the Information Systems Function." *Journal of Management Information Systems,* 1992, *8* (4), 63–82.

Society for Information Management Working Group on ISPA. *Information Systems Process Architecture 1.0.* Chicago: Society for Information Management, 1993.

Society for Information Management Working Group on ISPA. *Information Systems Process Architecture 2.0.* Chicago: Society for Information Management, 1996.

Society for Information Management Advanced Practices Council. *Practitioner's Guide to I. S. Performance Measurement.* Chicago: Society for Information Management, 1995.

Strassmann, P. A. *The Business Value of Computers.* New Canaan, Conn.: The Information Economics Press, 1990.

Strassmann, P. A., Berger, P., Burton Swanson, E., Kriebel, C. H., and Kauffman, R. J. *Measuring Business Value of Information Technologies.* Washington, D. C.: International Center for Information Technologies, 1988.

U.S. General Services Administration. *Performance-Based Management: Eight Steps to Develop and Use Information Technology Performance Measures Effectively.* Washington, D.C.: U.S. General Services Administration Office of Governmentwide Policy, 1996.

SHARON L. CAUDLE is a senior analyst with the U.S. General Accounting Office in Los Angeles.

An approach is presented in this chapter for providing performance measurement training for those who mandate, implement, and use performance measures. In addition to government roles, the level of experience and knowledge of the participants should drive the kind of training that is developed. Making this assessment requires an understanding of performance measurement systems and training applications.

Performance Measurement Training That Works

Cheryle A. Broom, Marilyn Jackson

To make government more performance-based, accountable, and cost-effective requires tools that the government participants can, and know how to, use. Training that provides those tools is critical but not easily found. One reason for this difficulty is that expectations can change and are evolving. Some agencies thought they were done with their reinvention efforts after reengineering their processes and becoming more customer-focused, using Osborne and Gaebler as their guides (Osborne and Gaebler, 1992). But policymakers took the concept further and directed agencies to establish standards of performance, to measure their actual performance against these standards, and to link their budget requests with program accomplishments (Congressional Budget Office, 1993; U.S. General Accounting Office, 1996). At the same time, as old programs naturally evolve and new ones are created, government agencies need training so that new techniques can be applied and old problems resolved.

Another challenge is to recognize that each state, county, local, and national unit of government has truly unique features. For example, when Oregon and Texas gained national attention for their statewide performance improvement programs, other states tried to replicate their models. They found that, although components could be used, each state must develop a program suitable to its situation (Broom and McGuire, 1995). Training should also be tailored to fit unique needs based on what stage the entity is in with establishing a performance measurement system and the trainees' role in the system. The training needs of the chair of a legislative committee are different from those of an agency supervisor. Different, too, are the needs of a budget analyst who has been using performance measures and the analyst who has no experience with performance measures. At any level, training must be practical and designed to help trainees move from lower to higher levels of knowledge, capability, confidence, and success in fulfilling their role.

We think training is particularly valuable when it is conducted by those with direct experience with performance measurement, a working knowledge of government operations, and a commitment to provide assistance directly applicable to the participants. Frequently, these trainers may be peers from another agency, jurisdiction, or professional organization. They know what is happening in the performance measurement arena and will work with the trainees to provide what is needed most to advance the trainees' performance measurement efforts. This includes follow-up mentoring and sharing of resources to benefit the performance movement across governmental boundaries.

Designing effective performance measurement training also requires the prerequisite skills in conducting training. This chapter focuses on the particulars of building a performance measurement training model for government. However, some readers may find it useful to gain more familiarity with communication and adult learning theories. In the case of instructional communications, trainers have to ensure that interaction is successful—or that messages are received and stored so they can be used when needed (Cohen, 1964; Schramm, 1972). Similarly, much has been written on creating learning environments for adults so trainees gain new knowledge and skills (Sims and Sims, 1991; Richey, 1992).

Finally, the kind of training we advocate practices principles of performance-based government: diagnose the situation, determine objectives and performance standards, develop and implement an efficient strategy or training approach, assess, and then follow up on the results. The remainder of this chapter offers our advice for performance measurement training that works.

Role in Government

Being involved in government, all trainees have something instantly in common. Their scope of authority and geographic location is not a divider so much as their individual role in government and their base of knowledge regarding performance measurement. Table 6.1 shows nine categories of trainees, each of which we think is best served by trainers who are sensitive to the on-the-job challenges they face, the purpose to which they need to put performance measurement, and their previous experience in developing or using performance measures. The matrix gives the trainer a baseline for developing a useful training program. However, this is a flexible classification system that merely provides guidance—the trainer will still need to address the unique needs and interests of each trainee.

The left column in the matrix lists three roles in government focused on in this chapter: agency staff, analysts, and policymakers—including top management. The next three columns suggest three types of knowledge and expe-

Table 6.1 Classification of Government Employees for Purposes of Performance Measurement Training

Role in Government	Existing Knowledge/Experience with Performance Measurement		
	Novice	Abstract	Applied
Agency Staff	1	2	3
Analysts	4	5	6
Policymakers	7	8	9

rience that trainees in each role are likely to have: novice-level, abstract, and applied.

Why dwell on these three roles? Because they represent the primary parties *within* government who are responsible for the way in which government actually runs—that is, performs. Agency staff include the spectrum of people who manage, administer, and provide service under policy mandates. Analysts review the agencies' budgets, policies, performance, and formal compliance with mandates. They make recommendations and advise policymakers within the agency and the legislative body who ultimately make the agency's work possible by allocating resources.

For a performance measurement system to work, these three roles must be effectively performed and linked. Many others are involved in the system, such as stakeholders, customers, contractors, and other entities. But policymakers, agency staff, and analysts are the leaders in mandating, implementing, and evaluating performance measures.

Acknowledging that all the trainees have at least heard about government performance improvement efforts, there will nonetheless be some with no direct experience with performance measurement. Their training needs will be more basic than those of their peers with the other two types of knowledge. These novices, regardless of their positions of authority, will need a context for understanding performance measurement and what it means for government.

Those with knowledge that is more abstract than applied will be looking for clarification of performance measurement concepts and practical assistance. At points 7 through 9 in Table 6.1, the reverse must be considered; that is, trainees may have developed or used performance measures but not fully understood why or how. They typically need guidance in addressing complications or concerns that have arisen when trying to use performance measures and reports.

Even then, agency staff, policymakers, and analysts with comparable knowledge of performance measurement will have some similar and some different interests. An experienced manager may be seeking some best practices or benchmarks that can used for measuring specific programs' results or ways to modify management information systems to incorporate new or different performance measures. The interest of the knowledgeable policymaker in the same jurisdiction may be on how to clarify policy intent so that programs put the emphasis on desired impacts and outcomes rather than assorted outputs. And the analyst with a fairly comprehensive understanding of performance measurement may be focused solely on how to incorporate performance measurement systems into budgets so that agencies' accomplishments can be linked to funding.

Context

Performance measurement training focuses on how to establish appropriate measures and track them. However, this is only a piece of the big picture. The training we advocate is conducted in the context of performance-based government or managing for results (U.S. General Accounting Office, 1996). Mandates and theories of performance-based government, strategic planning, performance budgeting, and performance assessment are four basic concepts that trainers should initially discuss, depending on trainees' role in government and acquaintance with performance measurement.

For all of the foregoing, the most worthy concepts and techniques, along with the most current understanding of what is working, should be discussed to some degree (American Society for Public Administration's Task Force on Government Accomplishment and Accountability, 1996). Explaining the linkages among the four subjects in Table 6.2 is particularly useful in providing a context for the trainees' efforts. Policymakers, especially, must understand the relationship of their efforts to the big picture of governance and accountability. For agency staff and analysts, performance measurement is largely a matter of implementation, but it can and should be used as a powerful tool to improve overall government performance.

Vocabulary

It is especially important for trainers to clearly define terms that have a specific meaning in performance measurement (but do not have a specific meaning in everyday usage), for example, the distinction between goals and objectives. Exhibit 6.1 presents the most important of these terms, which other trainers may use slightly differently. Our point is not to advance the detailed wording of each term, but to emphasize that trainees at any level, in any role, must be able to use the same basic vocabulary as trainers.

It might seem unnecessary to insist that trainees use terms in the same way as their trainers, but there is no other practical way to teach or discuss performance measurement. Similarly, trainees must share an understanding of the hierarchy governing the use of performance measurement terms. This hierarchy, illustrated in Figure 6.1, gives life to performance measurement terms and guides trainees in developing needed measurement systems. Otherwise trainees may be inclined to start with what is routinely done and then search to explain why. This, in the case of performance measurement, is

Table 6.2 Conveying the Broader Context of Performance Measurement to Trainees

Concept	Discussion Points
Policy Mandates and Theories	Federal mandates and programs—the Government Performance and Results Act, National Performance Review, and Chief Financial Officers Act
	Mandates/policies relevant to the jurisdiction/agency
	Current theories on performance management and measurement
Strategic Planning	Visions, missions, goals, and objectives
	Assessment of and strategies to achieve future role
	Development and use of appropriate performance measures
Performance Budgeting	Incorporating strategic plans and performance reporting in the budget development and monitoring process
	Roles, approaches, and system changes
Performance Assessment	How achievement of objectives is measured, tracked, reported, and evaluated
	Program evaluation and performance auditing
	Benchmarking/best practices
	Customer surveys and other tools

Exhibit 6.1 Performance Measurement Terms

Performance Measure	A quantifiable, enduring indicator of public sector outcomes, efficiency, or cost-effectiveness related to an entity's mission and programs, including the types of measures below
Outcome Measure (also known as effectiveness or impact)	The quantitative extent to which a service has achieved the entity's goals or objectives, met the needs of its clientele, or met commonly accepted professional standards
Cost-Effectiveness Measure	Expenditures per unit of outcome as defined above
Output Measure	The simple number of units produced, services provided, or people served by an entity or its programs
Efficiency Measure	Expenditures per unit of output as defined above

Figure 6.1. Hierarchy Governing Performance Reporting Concepts

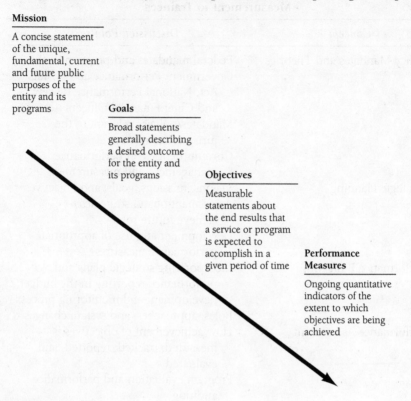

Mission

A concise statement
of the unique,
fundamental, current
and future public
purposes of the
entity and its
programs

Goals

Broad statements
generally describing
a desired outcome
for the entity and
its programs

Objectives

Measurable
statements about
the end results that
a service or program
is expected to
accomplish in a
given period of time

**Performance
Measures**

Ongoing quantitative
indicators of the
extent to which
objectives are being
achieved

backward and unproductive, resulting in scattered bits of information that are neither new nor instrumental to improving government.

Preliminaries

Trainers cannot assume that trainees will be ready to begin at a common point, although they may have much in common. On arrival at the training site, terms and concepts are much less important than gaining trainees' tacit agreement that they need the information that the session seeks to provide, government must manage itself more effectively and efficiently than it has in the past, and policymakers have a legitimate interest in the wise allocation of public resources—and that interest is served well by performance measures. There is no need to dwell on government's past problems; rather, trainers should fortify trainees' interest in doing better through performance measurement. The potential for certain weak programs being exposed by performance measurement should not be ignored, but rather acknowledged as one of several potentially painful truths that trainees may later face. Embarrassing as disclosure might be, such revelations could indeed be a sign of successful performance measurement.

Neither should trainees' mere appearance at performance measurement training sessions be interpreted to mean that they accept the tenets presented earlier or that they believe trainers are qualified. Trainers should present their qualifications in writing beforehand so no discussion on this topic is needed. More importantly, however, trainers should manifest the principles and practices of which they teach. So much the better if the trainers work in and for government yet have a measure of independence and autonomy. These characteristics, by adding to the trainers' credibility, generally increase trainees' willingness to endure the discomfort of their position as, in effect, pupils, as we discuss later.

The degree of trainees' psychological discomfort is generally proportionate to their usual degree of authority, past participation in government reform efforts, and current need for knowledge. These factors represent additional reasons to group trainees by their role in government and type of experience with performance measurement. There is little point in bogging down novices with veterans' potentially negative past experiences, nor in putting policymakers on the spot before subordinates.

Why all these preliminary considerations? It is a matter of measuring twice and cutting once (so to speak). In any event, such considerations occur up front and take little time once training sessions begin. Without thoughtful attention to preliminaries, trainers may find themselves plunging forward until near the end of the allotted time, only to have trainees pose what are by then unanswerable questions and concerns. Or sessions may go awry because trainees so often interrupt with interesting points of discussion.

We do not mean to suggest that trainers should be overbearing—in fact, the opposite is true. But it is essential that all participants "buy in" to the psychological exchange that is training. Following this buy-in, trainees need to be reinforced and rewarded with well-organized presentations and materials that they can put to use during and after the session. This includes a notebook or other collection of documents that mirror training topics, plus visual aids such as slides, transparencies, videotapes, handouts, and case studies.

In our experience, it works well to orchestrate sessions so that trainees have opportunities to approach the same concepts in different ways. Some learn better by listening and others by reading or doing. Whatever mode of learning is most appealing to trainers, they should use diverse methods of instruction. Also important are opportunities for trainees to verbalize what they have learned. Such opportunities, provided soon after points of instruction are made, can solidify understanding and help to bring learning to fruition.

Among other ways to encourage trainees to practice what they have learned, we ask small groups to review case studies and problem scenarios, then designate a reporter who offers their observations to the larger group. Short, casual, self-scored quizzes at various points also help trainees as well as trainers to become aware of knowledge gaps and ambiguities.

It goes without saying that trainees always should be accorded respect, good humor, and frequent breaks. Breaks bring closure to topics while allowing trainees to pursue questions individually, among themselves, or with trainers.

Training Needs Based on Role in Government

Agency line staff, analysts, and elected officials view performance measurement from very different perspectives. Their information needs differ, as do their training needs.

Agency Staff. Of the three types of government workers we have identified, agency staff face the greatest number of performance measurement tasks. They not only must develop performance objectives, and the measures themselves, but also collect and maintain performance data, continue to run government programs while changing procedures in order to improve performance, communicate progress or the lack of it, and be prepared for favorable or unfavorable reactions.

Under these circumstances, it is important for trainers to take a constructive stance that emphasizes the advantage that performance measures bring despite the difficulties they may pose. Of these, perhaps the strongest cases to be made are that performance measures are better points of discussion than line items in a budget and that agency staff have an opportunity to set the agenda for discussion with policymakers as they identify objectives, performance targets, and measures.

At the novice point, agency staff need assistance in identifying and translating their agency's mission statements into goals, their agency's broad goals into program performance objectives, and objectives into performance measures. They must also be made aware of the need to check for consistency between statutes and their stated mission and goals. Missions, vision statements, and strategic plans sometimes are developed by the executive branch without legislative input.

For agency staff with a base of knowledge about performance measurement, trainers should move quickly beyond terms and concepts, turning attention to the specifics of objectives, measures, information gathering, and reporting systems. We find it especially helpful to introduce well-crafted, actual examples of objectives and measures that are in use within other government programs. The more relevant these examples are to the programs that agency staff run, the better. Also, by way of contrast, some poorly crafted examples can be useful.

For agency staff who have developed or used performance data without a strong conceptual foundation, trainers should focus first on unraveling the logical connections among missions, goals, objectives, and measures. Second, the topic of measurement should be addressed, particularly its strengths, limitations, and purpose. In this case, the purpose is primarily to inform policymakers not to operate programs.

Agency staff at any level should be made aware of the distinction between information needed for the day-to-day business of running government and information needed for evaluating programs. This can be confusing, because computerized systems demand much raw information, but only some of their output bears on program results. Other detailed information might be useful for management. The dilemma for agency staff is how to select a few practical performance indicators per program and continue to use them despite minor imperfections. Otherwise, they may inadvertently subvert their own and others' efforts to track performance.

Analysts. Government analysts can be among those most amenable to performance measurement training but must guard against being hypercritical. Often, they have completed at least some helpful coursework, such as statistics and research design. They also tend to be comfortable with computerized databases and numbers. Unfortunately, analysts may have such detailed knowledge that they have a hard time seeing the big picture, as discussed earlier. Another potential problem is that analysts may be biased against customer surveys and other sources of nonfinancial data. Also, trainers must be aware that government analysts may have developed positive or negative preconceptions about government programs and agency staff.

We suggest that trainers initially engage analysts in a discussion of measurement that includes the points mentioned above but also extends to the topic of what constitutes performance measures. Ideally, these are quantifiable, enduring indicators of the extent to which performance objectives are achieved. For example, "development of a statewide plan by 2000" is barely quantifiable (yes/no) and at best is a one-time phenomenon.

Next, trainers should explain in some detail how to evaluate performance measures. Such evaluation may be surprisingly difficult because analysts must determine whether

- Measures directly relate to agencies' objectives and goals
- Measures concern the same phenomena consistently over time
- Data have been, or will be, routinely available without inordinate new costs
- Agencies have taken, or will take, some action that impacts upon the target group or problem

For analysts who are novices at performance measurements, trainers especially need to help them discriminate the different types of performance measures in Exhibit 6.1. For analysts with abstract knowledge of performance measurement, we suggest that analysts try their hand at actually developing some performance measures for their own or other familiar organizations. And for analysts with only applied knowledge of performance measures, training should allow time for discussion of the political, economic, and social context that has led to worldwide enthusiasm for performance measurement systems.

Policymakers. Public officials may be anxious to embrace performance measurement as a direct link to improving the bottom line. Alternatively, they may be skeptical that any such strategy can improve or should change the way they make decisions. To address the needs of policymakers necessitates surveying the political environment from their vantage point. Does a key elected official, party, or leadership group want to change things? If so, why? Is performance measurement seen as one of the potential avenues to achieve a social or political policy objective?

Our observation is that policymakers run the gamut of understandings and attitudes toward performance measurement and their participation in it. Irrespective of the point their jurisdictions have reached in measures, policymakers in training are likely to offer their own perspectives. Trainers need to get those perspectives on the table early so that sessions can move forward appropriately. As mentioned in the introduction, understanding adult learning behavior is important (Wells, Layne, and Allen, 1991; Craig, 1994).

Items of particular interest to policymakers include

- How their jurisdiction has measured or has tried to measure its performance
- How similar jurisdictions have approached performance measurement
- How policymakers have been involved
- What can be achieved, the risks involved, and successful implementation strategies
- How to fulfill their role and help to achieve goals envisioned for their jurisdiction
- How to incorporate agency performance measures in policymaking

The realities as well as the benefits of performance measurement should be covered in some detail. For example, policymakers at the novice level of performance measurement may expect a straightforward system that provides performance data clearly linked to agency missions and budgets. They may also envision ready information about what it costs to produce a given level and quality of service so that budget allocation decisions become easier. This simplistic example illustrates a problem with explaining performance measurement. Busy public officials want quick and easy answers as to what works best and what costs the least. Although performance measurement can certainly help them find answers, the process is more complicated and requires that they delve deeper into it. Training should help policymakers take this plunge and show them what they can expect to get and use depending on the jurisdiction's performance measurement system. This also provides an opportunity for policymakers to assess ways they can influence the performance measurement system.

For policymakers new to their jobs or to this concept, the aforementioned training or education program may be fairly straightforward. If seasoned officials are the primary audience, trainers must take a different tack. As performance measurement experts, trainers serve more as facilitators. They develop a strategy with the participants that includes using performance measurement to help trainees meet their priorities.

Finally, for policymakers with limited knowledge and experience, a training program should be developed that falls somewhere in between the other two approaches. Trainers are challenged to ensure that solid groundwork has been laid while helping the participants to formulate plans for pursuing their intent. For example, a fiscal committee chair may need ideas for preparing his or her committee to review and use aggregate performance information that is provided in the budget process. The governor, on the other hand, may seek measures that help her or him to show the public and other policymakers that a major new program initiative is working or tangibly achieving its desired results. Again, these are the higher-level measures relating to meeting the juris-diction's and agencies' missions. Policymakers do not typically need to know the mechanics of an agency's performance measurement system. Trainers work-ing with them will find their plates sufficiently full without overlapping into the duties of administrators and evaluators.

Performance Measurement Training Helps Improve Public Programs

Using performance measurement to improve public programs requires lead-ership, knowledge, and understanding how to achieve performance measure-ment objectives. Training can help meet these requirements. Effective training focuses on the information needs of each group of trainees.

Training by Role in Government. Our performance measurement train-ing model focuses on working with three key groups in government and pro-viding them training based on their level of knowledge or experience.

Our approach stems from observing a rather poor fit between many trainees' needs and the executive branch's initial efforts to train employees of Washington State and Minnesota in performance measurement. Both states began with large-scale, general training and later discovered that small-scale sessions, specific to government employees' needs, were more effective.

We show that agency staff need to know how to develop, implement, and monitor performance measures for their organization. Performance measure-ment management features, such as developing valid instruments to evaluate customer satisfaction and tracking systems that provide reliable performance data, are emphasized.

Analysts have some interests in common with agency staff in terms of understanding how to develop a good performance measure. Further, budget analysts and program evaluators need to know how to assess the appropriate-ness of performance measures developed by agencies and how to relate agency measures to the objectives and mandates of public officials.

Members of our last group, policymakers, typically have a broader inter-est than the other two. They need grounding in what constitutes a good per-formance measurement system in the context of public policy to improve the performance and accountability of government. Delving into the techniques of developing and using measures at the program or operational level is unnecessary. However, policymakers typically need training on formulating the jurisdiction, or program policy, level of measures as well as some guidance on how to meet their objectives related to measuring the performance of government.

Training by Type of Knowledge. The other feature of our training approach is to consider the type of knowledge participants have in performance measurement. Novices need a different emphasis than those with experience in applying the concept. Those in between may have an abstract understanding of the concepts, but not the ability to effectively use them. Our approach promotes training based on the user's role *and* understanding, recognizing that ultimately the training will be further crafted around the specific needs or objectives of the participants.

Conclude with Training's Value. As evidenced by our suggestions, we promote performance measurement training that is directed at meeting the needs of the policymakers, agency staff, and government analysts. We have shown in this chapter the type of training program and instructor who can meet these needs. Our experience is that the model outlined in this chapter can help make performance measurement work in government. We anticipate that readers who use our approach will experience a similar outcome.

References

American Society for Public Administration's Task Force on Government Accomplishment and Accountability. Case Studies distributed at the 1996 National ASPA Training Conference, Atlanta, Ga., June 30–July 2, 1996.

Broom, C. A., and McGuire, L. A. "Performance-Based Government Models: Building a Track Record." *Public Budgeting and Finance,* Winter 1995, *15* (4), 3–17.

Cohen, A. R. *Attitude Change and Social Influence.* New York: Basic Books, 1964.

Congressional Budget Office. *Using Performance Measures in the Federal Budget Process.* Washington, D.C.: U.S. Government Printing Office, 1993.

Craig, M. *Analyzing Learning Needs.* Hampshire, England: Gower Publishing Limited, 1994.

Osborne, D., and Gasbler, T. *Reinventing Government.* Reading, Mass.: Addison-Wesley, 1992.

Richey, R. *Designing Instruction for the Adult Learner.* London: Kogan Page Limited, 1992.

Schramm, W. (ed.). *The Process and the Facts of Mass Communication.* (2nd ed.) Urbana, Ill.: University of Illinois Press, 1972.

Sims, R. R., and Sims, S. A. "Improving Training in the Public Sector." *Public Personnel Management,* Spring 1991, *20* (1), 71–83.

U.S. General Accounting Office. *Effectively Implementing the Government Performance and Results Act.* Washington, D.C.: U.S. General Accounting Office, 1996.

Wells, J. B., Layne, B. H., and Allen, D. "Management Development Training and Learning Styles." *Public Productivity and Management Review,* Spring 1991, *14,* (4), 415–428.

CHERYLE A. BROOM *is the legislative auditor for the Washington State Joint Legislative Audit and Review Committee.*

MARILYN JACKSON *is an evaluation coordinator in the State of Minnesota, Office of the Legislative Auditor.*

The evaluation profession has been affected by two crises during the last two decades: the evaluation crisis, characterized by a deficit in evaluation utilization, and a more important governance crisis, characterized by deficits in government performance and credibility. Tactics and tools for evaluators to use in addressing these challenges are described in this chapter, and recommendations are offered for evaluators and program managers to better define, measure, and improve government performance.

Clarifying Goals, Reporting Results

Joseph S. Wholey, Kathryn E. Newcomer

Over the last twenty years, the evaluation profession has been affected by two crises: an evaluation crisis, characterized by a deficit in evaluation utilization, and a more important governance crisis, characterized by deficits in government performance and credibility. Responses to the two crises are intertwined.

This chapter reviews problems in ensuring evaluation utilization and in measuring government performance, explores how evaluators can help solve these problems, and presents lessons learned from government experience with performance measurement and evaluation. Recommendations are then offered to encourage evaluators' involvement in current efforts to define, measure, and improve government performance.

Increasing Evaluation Utilization: Evaluability Assessment

In the mid-1970s, the lack of utilization of evaluation findings became evident at all levels of government. Evaluators were pushed to rethink their approach to offering information about the performance of public programs. A team from the Urban Institute concluded that the underlying problems inhibiting utilization of evaluation include the following: evaluators and intended users may not agree on the goals, objectives, and performance criteria to be used in evaluating programs; program goals and objectives may be unrealistic, given the resources that have been committed to them and the program activities that are under way; relevant information on program performance may be unavailable or may not be obtainable at a reasonable cost; and policymakers and managers may be unable or unwilling to use evaluation information in making decisions about the program (Horst, Nay, Scanlon, and Wholey, 1974; Wholey, Hatry, and Newcomer, 1994).

The team suggested a process—*evaluability assessment*—that would overcome these problems by involving managers and other key stakeholders in four

NEW DIRECTIONS FOR EVALUATION, no. 75, Fall 1997 © Jossey-Bass Publishers steps during the evaluation design phase: developing at least implicit agreement on program design, including the resources allocated to the program, intended program activities, expected program outputs, expected program outcomes, and assumed causal linkages among inputs, activities, outputs, and outcomes; developing agreement on any changes in program design needed to ensure that program goals and objectives are plausible; developing agreement on appropriate measures of program inputs, program activities, program outputs, and program outcomes; and developing agreement on evaluation priorities and intended uses of evaluation information.

Evaluability assessment uses logic models to display the programmatic components. The logic models identify the resources allocated to the program, intended program activities, expected program outputs and outcomes, and assumed causal linkages among inputs, activities, outputs, and outcomes, as seen by managers, policymakers, and other key stakeholders affected by or interested in the program. The process can help highlight differences in expectations among different stakeholders and facilitate agreement between evaluators and the intended users of evaluation information on what constitutes the intended program. Examination of the logic models developed by evaluators can help stakeholders develop agreement on the relevant dimensions in terms of which programs might be evaluated and on performance measures and evaluation priorities before further evaluation work is undertaken.

The evaluability assessment process often results in identification of intermediate outcomes that connect program activities to program goals and that can be measured to evaluate programmatic performance. Evaluability assessment can be especially helpful in clarifying intended uses of evaluation information to improve program performance and to communicate the value of program activities to policy levels.

For over two decades evaluators have viewed evaluability assessment as a tool that can be used when evaluations or performance measurement systems are being designed. This process can be used to ensure that subsequent analytical work will focus on relevant performance dimensions, will use appropriate performance measures, and will produce useful performance information.

Embracing Performance Measurement

The governance crisis that has ballooned over the last two decades has turned the attention of program managers and government oversight actors to some of the same issues that evaluators have been addressing in their quest for improving government programs through development of relevant evaluation data. The current focus on performance measurement at all levels of government and in nonprofit organizations reflects citizen demands for evidence or program effectiveness that have been made around the world. Rising budget deficits and decreasing public confidence have pressured governments in most developed countries to respond with performance data.

The Government Performance and Results Act of 1993 echoes the intent of other governments within the United States as well as abroad in its call for program managers to use planning and performance measurement to improve the confidence of the American people in the capability of the federal government by systematically holding federal agencies accountable for achieving program results; improve federal program effectiveness and public accountability by promoting a new focus on results, service quality, and customer satisfaction; help federal managers improve service delivery by requiring that they plan for meeting program objectives and by providing more objective information on achieving statutory objectives and on the relative effectiveness and efficiency of federal programs and spending; and improve internal management of the federal government (Government Performance and Results Act, Section 2).

The Act requires agency leaders to explore the expectations and priorities of Congress and other key stakeholders, and chart a course for the future that identifies agency mission, strategic goals and objectives, and implementation strategies to achieve the objectives. The agencies are required to develop strategic plans and revise them every three years and to identify performance measures and annual performance targets for agency programs. Planning and performance measurement are the tools that are to be used to help agencies manage their programs and communicate their successes to the outside world more effectively.

The theory behind the Government Performance and Results Act is that planning and performance measurement will help agencies communicate performance expectations and results—and that the use of performance information will improve management and program effectiveness, improve policy decision making, and improve public confidence in government. Implicit in the theory underlying the Act are two additional assumptions: the necessary levels of political, management, and analytical support for planning and performance measurement will materialize, and managers and policymakers will use performance information if it is made available.

Using Performance Measurement to Improve Government Performance: Some Lessons Learned from Federal Agency Experience

Utilization of performance data is a critical concern for those struggling to implement the Government Performance and Results Act at the federal level, just as it is for managers implementing similar directives at state and local levels of government (Epstein and Olsen, 1996; Newcomer and Wright, 1996). Initial experiences with performance measurement suggest that program managers and evaluators face many challenges in facilitating effective utilization of performance measurement systems.

Implementation of the Government Performance and Results Act began with a set of pilot projects in performance planning and reporting in fiscal years 1994–1996, with governmentwide implementation set for 1997. Although only ten performance measurement pilot projects were required under the law, federal agencies reacted with considerable enthusiasm, implementing approximately seventy performance measurement pilot projects covering more than 450,000 staff members and almost every budget function of the federal government. Efforts to review the experience of the pilots have been undertaken by the U.S. General Accounting Office (1994, 1995, 1996, and 1997) and the National Academy of Public Administration (1994, 1997), among others. Some lessons learned by managers in the pilots are instructive for performance measurement in any governmental or nonprofit context.

First, top leadership support is clearly the critical element that can make or break strategic planning and performance measurement efforts. The key finding of virtually all observers of performance measurement efforts is that the support of agency leadership is essential to ensure the success of the system. The current challenge many line managers face is that there is inadequate understanding and buy-in among agency leadership. Both moral support and resources are crucial to ensure that performance measurement becomes real and not simply a paper exercise. If agency leaders simply give the Act lip service, chances are that line managers will, as well. If political appointees do not support the immense efforts that managers will need to expend to collect and use performance data, any movement toward results-oriented management is doomed, and if managers in the field do not perceive that headquarters supports their efforts in this regard, the results will be nil.

A key indicator of top leadership support is the commitment of resources—including the time of top level managers—to the design and implementation of useful performance measurement systems. For example, the Assistant Secretary for Children and Families at the U.S. Department of Health and Human Services made her intense advocacy of performance measurement clear from the time of her appointment in 1993, and her agenda showed it. Her support for the performance measurement pilot in the Child Support Enforcement Agency was critical to the office's ability to devise performance measures acceptable to key constituencies. Listening to stakeholders whose input is critical to development of measures takes time. Collaborating with state child support enforcement officials on the development of performance measures and targets took a great deal of staff time. The staff time, requisite information technology, and other development costs present hefty investments that are only available when top level support exists.

Second, the personal involvement of senior line managers is critical. Senior line managers must be involved in the planning process. Performance measures must be relevant and useful to line management. The Government Performance and Results Act was intended to empower program managers to participate in the development of the program mission statement, goals, and performance indicators. With the involvement of agency chief financial officers, agency budget staff, and Office of Management and Budget (OMB) examiners, it should not be surprising that there can be confusion over the ownership of this process. The issue of where stewardship over the performance measurement process is located is important. In some agencies policy staff members are working on strategic plans, and the chief financial officer's staff members are working on the performance measures. In other agencies, such as the Treasury Department, a comprehensive planning office linked to the budget office is undertaking the entire planning and performance measurement effort. Who takes responsibility for performance measurement clearly matters. If control over the process is located in financial management offices, it may be difficult to ensure that measures are line manager-friendly. If the budget office develops measures specifically to accompany and support budget requests, it is very likely that the measures will not serve line managers' internal needs. Also, if there is not buy-in by the line managers who play key roles in data collection, serious problems may ensue.

Third, participation of the relevant stakeholders is needed to develop useful plans and performance measures. Consultation with Congress on the development of strategic plans is a statutory requirement of the Act that is raising expectations that Congress may become more involved in internal agency decision making. Securing a reasonable level of agreement on appropriate strategic objectives and relevant performance measures among stakeholders within the agency; within other offices in the Executive Branch, such as OMB; in the states (for the many intergovernmental programs); and the Congress presents an especially impressive challenge. Engaging congressional committees in programmatic matters outside of the authorization and appropriation processes is not routine; thus, some experience is needed to assure agency staff that the required consultation will not open them to micro-management. So far there are no models to shape expectations on either side. However, securing agreement from congressional stakeholders on strategic planning and performance targets could actually reduce opportunities for reactive micro-management.

Fourth, technical assistance in the design of useful performance measurement systems is often necessary but may not be available when needed. OMB initially emerged as the prime mover in urging federal managers to develop performance measures, but there have been complaints about the assistance that OMB has provided agencies as they struggle to develop appropriate performance measures and measurement systems. On the one hand, OMB is urging creativity and recognizing that diversity across programs in the sorts of measures they use may be appropriate. On the other hand, agency staff accustomed to following OMB directives may find themselves uncertain as to what measures are best.

Fifth, uncertainty about how performance data will be used will inhibit the design of useful performance measurement systems. The current fervor for budget cuts has sent an important message to managers coping with demands for performance report cards: systematic performance measurement could provide useful data to inform budget cutting. Recognition that performance data could be used against them could send the message to program managers that the measures they develop had better make their programs look good.

The dilemma about different uses for performance data presents what is perhaps the most difficult challenge to developing performance measurement systems that will support management decision making. Given the initially heavy involvement of financial management and budget offices in federal performance measurement efforts, data that will best support budgetary requests tend to be selected over performance measures that may be more helpful for internal managerial uses.

Experience within the Act's pilot projects has revealed how challenging it is to secure agreement within agencies on the selection of performance measures. The level of dialogue about the differences between program inputs, outputs, and outcomes has shown that there are very different views held by agency staff about what should be measured and how the measures should be used.

As a related matter, there is anxiety within agency staff about measuring outcomes to evaluate program effectiveness when the measures may well be used for resource allocation purposes. In so many programs, from providing job training to welfare mothers to increasing armed forces capabilities to prevent the outbreak of war, it is difficult to establish a causal link between the government effort and the eventual outcome for the individual or society served. In some cases it is simply impossible to measure programmatic outcomes in the sort of real time that the Act envisions. For example, programs intended to prevent war, homelessness, or the spread of AIDS are unlikely to be able to develop annual performance data to guide either internal or oversight decision making.

On the positive side, there are documented instances among federal performance measurement pilots that measures have been developed and used. Internal management improvement has been accomplished through using performance measures in several ways. First, agreement on performance measures has helped to tighten lines of communication about performance expectations in some agencies. For example, the National Highway Traffic Safety Administration, the Healthy People program in the Department of Health and Human Services, the Chesapeake Bay Program in the Environmental Protection Agency, and the Coast Guard have all used performance measures to improve program effectiveness through clarifying expectations with key partners. With the large number of intergovernmental programs requiring the cooperative efforts of multiple public and nonprofit agencies, the use of performance measures to facilitate coordination is no mean feat.

Second, internal reallocation of resources has been attributed to the use of performance measurement systems in a number of agencies, as well, including the Coast Guard, the Army Audit Agency, the Inter-American Foundation, the Chesapeake Bay program, the Energy Information Administration, and the Highway Traffic Safety Administration. The Coast Guard reports basing reallocation decisions on performance data, noting, "Our line managers in the field use the measures in our Business Plan and quarterly data extracts to help target their activities toward goal achievement, based on local risks. . . . By using outcome information in managing our programs, we met or exceeded seven of eight ambitious targets for safety and environmental protection in our first year, and five of seven in our second year, with no additional resources" (U.S. Coast Guard, 1996, pp. 8, 10).

Third, heightened awareness among employees about the need to be outcome-oriented has been reported in many agencies. More frequent use of customer surveys and internal distribution of survey results, along with strategic plans, business plans, and performance measures, has sensitized employees to the need to be outcome-oriented as they plan and implement activities. Reports of the positive effects of this heightened awareness come from the National Air and Space Administration, the Coast Guard, the Army Audit Agency, and the Energy Information Administration. For example, in the Energy

Information Administration, management reports that line managers proposing projects know they must include outcome measures with their plans.

Fourth, incentives to reward high performers—as measured by newly devised performance measures—have also been used in some agencies. For example, high-performing Public Housing Authorities coordinated by the Department of Housing and Urban Development have received benefits in the form of reduced paperwork requirements and public accolades. The Healthy People Program in the Department of Health and Human Services has also recognized and publicized best practices demonstrated by high-performing units in the Public Health Service.

Turning to the use of performance measures for external resource negotiations, virtually all federal agencies have been submitting performance measures with budgetary requests. There have been reports of successful use of performance data to defend against budget cuts, and even to increase allocations. The Army Audit Agency reports that it was able to use its performance data to reduce a proposed FY96 budget cut of $10 million in half. The Coast Guard reports that it was able to use its performance data to increase its FY95 appropriation by $5 million, with Senate report language citing the importance of the program goals and its Business Plan as the rationale (U.S. Coast Guard, 1996).

Philip Joyce rightly identifies many obstacles to moving toward performance-based budgeting, in Chapter Four of this volume, and there is not much evidence to suggest a systematic shift in budgeting caused by the provision of performance measures. However, performance measurement offers the potential to be used in an ad hoc fashion to defend against proposed cuts, as the cases here illustrate.

There are many opportunities open to managers who embrace performance measurement as a means to improve programs operations. The challenge is to move managers and management systems into positions where they can take advantage of these opportunities.

Applying Evaluation Expertise to Promote Performance Measurement

Designing and implementing performance measurement systems that will provide data on how well programs track against the agency's mission is politically challenging and resource-intensive. There are many challenges to ensuring that performance measurement serves agency management and the public, and the evaluation profession can help program managers meet these challenges.

Securing agreement among the key stakeholders regarding agency mission and strategic objectives is the first step. If performance measures do not tie in with strategic objectives, it will be difficult to use them to manage effectively. Clarifying program goals is a task with which evaluators are quite familiar. The evaluability assessment process discussed previously was developed for this task. Effectively involving the relevant stakeholders and securing a reasonable level of consensus on desired program outcomes and appropriate measures of such results are types of support that evaluators can offer to program managers.

Evaluators have knowledge and communication skills to serve program managers by helping to educate and sensitize top agency management on the

benefits of results-oriented management and the design and support requirements of useful performance measurement systems. Evaluators also possess
the technical expertise needed to inform the design of performance measurement systems as well as the analysis of performance data.

Identifying and communicating the reasons that programs do not perform
at expected levels is also clearly the province of program evaluation. Performance measurement alone will typically not provide the data that program
managers need to understand why performance is below expectations, nor will
it tell them how they may improve operations. The wide variety of program
evaluation techniques that can be used to illuminate program operations com-
plements performance measurement.

Evaluators have skills that are needed to support managers who are now
working to define realistic goals, develop output and outcome measures, report
results, and use information on goals and results to improve management, program effectiveness, policy decision making, and public trust. We hope and
expect that the evaluation profession will be involved in helping to meet these
emerging public management challenges.

References

Epstein, J., and Olsen, R. T. "Lessons Learned by State and Local Governments," *The Pub-
lic Manager,* Fall 1996, pp. 41–44.
Horst, P., Nay, J. N., Scanlon, J. W., and Wholey, J. S. "Program Management and the Fed-
eral Evaluator." *Public Administration Review,* 1974, *34* (4), 300–308.
National Academy of Public Administration. *The Government Performance and Result Act: Early
Implementation.* Washington, D.C.: National Academy of Public Administration, 1994.
National Academy of Public Administration. *Implementing the Results Act.* Washington, D.C.:
National Academy of Public Administration, forthcoming, 1997.
Newcomer, K. E., and Wright, R. E. "Managing for Outcomes: Federal Uses for Performance
Measurement." *The Public Manager,* 1996, 25 (4), 31–36.
U.S. Coast Guard. *Using Outcome Information to Redirect Programs: A Case Study of the Coast
Guard's Pilot Project Under the Government Performance and Results Act.* 1996.
U.S. General Accounting Office. *Managing for Results: State Experiences Provide Insights for Federal Man-
agement Reform.* GAO/GGD-95-22. Washington, D.C.: U.S. General Accounting Office, 1994.
U.S. General Accounting Office. *Managing for Results: Experiences Abroad Suggest Insights for Federal
Management Reform.* GAO/GGD-95-20. Washington, D.C.: U.S. General Accounting Office, 1995.
U.S. General Accounting Office. *Executive Guide: Effectively Implementing the Government Performance
and Results Act.* GAO/GGD-96-118. Washington, D.C.: U.S. General Accounting Office, 1996.
U.S. General Accounting Office. *Managing for Results: Using GPRA to Assist Congressional and
Executive Branch Decisionmaking.* GAO/T-GGD-97-43. Washington, D.C.: U.S. General
Accounting Office, 1997.
Wholey, J. S., Hatry, H. P., and Newcomer, K. E. (eds.). *Handbook of Practical Program Eval-
uation.* San Francisco: Jossey-Bass, 1994.

JOSEPH S. WHOLEY *is a professor at the University of Southern California's Public
Affairs Center in Washington, D.C.*

KATHRYN E. NEWCOMER *is a professor and the department chair in the Department
of Public Administration, The George Washington University, Washington, D.C.*

INDEX

Ordering Information

New Directions for Evaluation is a series of paperback books that presents the latest techniques and procedures for conducting useful evaluation studies of all types of programs. Books in the series are published quarterly in Spring, Summer, Fall, and Winter and are available for purchase by subscription as well as by single copy.

Subscriptions cost $63.00 for individuals (a savings of 28 percent over single-copy prices) and $105.00 for institutions, agencies, and libraries. Please do not send institutional checks for personal subscriptions. Standing orders are accepted. Prices subject to change. (For subscriptions outside of North America, add $7.00 for shipping via surface mail or $25.00 for air mail. Orders *must be prepaid* in U.S. dollars by check drawn on a U.S. bank or charged to VISA, MasterCard, or American Express.)

Single copies cost $22.00 plus shipping (see below) when payment accompanies order. California, New Jersey, New York, and Washington, D.C., residents please include appropriate sales tax. Canadian residents add GST and any local taxes. Billed orders will be charged shipping and handling. No billed shipments to post office boxes. (Orders from outside North America *must be prepaid* in U.S. dollars by check drawn on a U.S. bank or charged to VISA, MasterCard, or American Express.)

Shipping (Single Copies Only): $30.00 and under, add $5.50; to $50.00, add $6.50; to $75.00, add $7.50; to $100, add $9.00; to $150.00, add $10.00.

Discounts for quantity orders are available. Please write to the address below for information.

All orders must include either the name of an individual or an official purchase order number. Please submit your order as follows:
 Subscriptions: specify series and year subscription is to begin
 Single copies: include individual title code (such as PE59)

Mail orders to:
 Jossey-Bass Publishers
 350 Sansome Street
 San Francisco, California 94104-1342

Phone subscription or single-copy orders toll-free at (888) 378-2537 or at (415) 433-1767 (toll call).

Fax orders toll-free to: (800) 605-2665

For subscription sales outside of the United States, contact
 any international subscription agency or Jossey-Bass directly.